THAT I MIGHT KNOW HIM

Spiritual Food
For Spiritual Growth

BOOK 1

NANCY TAYLOR TATE

That I Might Know Him

Spiritual Food for Spiritual Growth

Nancy Taylor Tate

First Edition

First printing September 2022

COPYRIGHT © 2022

Nancy Taylor Tate

Contact Information for Nancy Taylor Tate can be found on our ministry website:

www.wadetaylor.org

Deeper Life Press

Contents

Acknowledgements

Thank You,
Lord, for Your faithfulness, love, and enabling grace
With appreciation,
I acknowledge and ask that You bless

Allen Tate, my husband and best friend, joined in heart, calling, purpose, and ministry.

Sharon Whitby, my niece, who is an awesome editor and fun to work with.

Steve Porter, our friend, who encouraged and helped us publish these books.

Prayer Partners, Friends, and Family who have made a difference in my life.

Dedication

I dedicate this book with love to Joe Wade, my son,
and to his family

In Loving Memory of

David, my husband until the Lord took him home, for
his love, faith, and prayers

Wade Taylor, my dad, for truths he shared, impacting
my life and walk with the Lord

Section 1
The Faithfulness of God

"God is faithful, by whom you were called unto the fellowship of his Son Jesus Christ our Lord." 1 Corinthians 1:9

I n this book are words written over a lifetime, expressing spiritual life-giving truths that have changed my life and have blessed many others along the way. As my husband Allen and I put this book together, it has been quite an experience for me. Each section brought back memories of times in the presence of the Lord and of His working in my life.

A spiritual truth I have based my life decisions on for many years is found in the verse below:

"I love them that love me; and those that seek me early shall find me." Proverbs 8:17

Here, the Lord is speaking of His love for those who love Him. He agapes, or loves unconditionally, the whole world (John 3:16). But there is that in the heart of God that responds to those who love Him (Proverbs 8:17).

In the same verse, the Lord promises that those who seek Him early, or who make Him a priority, will find Him. What a wonderful promise as we set the poise of our spirit toward Him, that we might seek Him with all of our heart.

I can think of nothing better to have in this life than the favor of the Lord resting upon us. This is the blessing the Lord promises to those who seek after Him.

"Blessed is the man that heareth me, watching daily at my gates, waiting at the posts of my doors. For whoso findeth me findeth life, and shall obtain favour of the LORD." Proverbs 8:34-35

Even more, I see the faithfulness of God. In 1981 the Lord called me to support my dad, Wade Taylor, in his ministry. For years I served in a variety of places, wherever I was needed. I soon realized I was not called just to support a person, but a vision – the preparation of a people for the end-time purposes of the Lord – and it burns deep in my heart today.

What follows are teachings that sow into that vision and that also changed my life. My prayer is that these truths will encourage and strengthen you, as you too continue to grow in your walk and relationship with the Lord Jesus Christ.

Many scriptures are included. Jesus said, *"the words I speak ... are spirit and ... life"* (John 6:63). Our prayer is that as you read, there will be an impartation of spirit and life that will feed you spiritually.

God loves each one of us and created us with a purpose in mind. My prayer is that you will see the love of God in your life in a fresh, new way. His heart toward you, and also His working, is to turn that which in the natural or worldly sense is "not so good," into something "good" inside of you, of eternal value.

May the Lord bless you through these writings. As you identify the truths being expressed, I encourage you to pray into them, applying them to your life experiences as you invite the Lord to work deep within your heart.

This book is best read devotionally, one chapter at a time. Each chapter is complete of itself. Some sections are longer than others. Take your time and allow the Word to get into your spirit. Pray the scriptures!

You are *special* to Him! He has a plan and a purpose for your life. You will see as you read on that it is what we are "becoming" even more than what we "do" that Christ is interested in.

Our prayer is that the truths in this book will encourage the reproduction of Christ in a many-membered body. *"Christ in you, the hope of glory"* (Colossians 1:27b). Christ in us, a greater glory!

Below is a heartfelt prayer for the Lord's further touch, that you too might want to express to the Lord, as we continue reading:

Father, I ask that as I reflect on these truths, You would touch my heart and change my life, drawing me ever closer to You. Thank You, Lord, for Your hand on my life. In Jesus' name I pray, Amen.

Christ in me —
the hope of
glory ♡

touch my heart,
change my life,
draw me closer
to You ♡

Section 2
Our First Priority

A Revelation of a Relationship

"He that eateth me, even he shall live by me."
John 6:57

Establishing and maintaining a close personal relationship with our Lord and Saviour, Jesus Christ, should be central to our spiritual life and ministry. We may be satisfied that we are seeking a deeper understanding of the Word of God. Still, it is essential also that we go beyond this level of spiritual desire and recognize that the only foundation upon which our knowledge of the Word can stand is the personal relationship that we maintain with the Lord.

16

The Lord greatly desires to further make Himself known to us. Most certainly, we are to seek after His anointing and the operation of gifts in our ministries. However, before there can be a quality impartation of "spirit and life" to others through the operation of these ministries and gifts, there must first be developed within us a quality of spirit which comes only from our having a personal knowledge of the Lord.

Through learning to live in His presence, and also spending quality time alone with Him, there will come a deposit of "spirit and life" in our own lives. From that deposit within there will come a spiritual impartation, beyond our words as we minister to others.

For us to be willing to spend these extended times of waiting in His presence, there must first be within us a "dissatisfied satisfaction." We are to be satisfied with all that we have of the Lord and His workings within our lives, but we must become dissatisfied, knowing that there is much more to be gained in our knowledge of Him. There must be a genuine fervor in our seeking, as we hunger after an increased, inward, personal knowledge of Him.

As we come in anticipation and wait in His presence, He will begin to reveal to us the obstacles which hinder our relationship to Him, and impart to us the grace to deal with them. It is only the goodness of the Lord and His patience toward us that brings us to repentance, calling us to holiness, a life consecrated to Him.

As we continue setting apart time to linger in His presence and grow in this consecrated walk, the reflection of the glory which comes from our being in His presence will begin to change us into His image. Even as Moses reflected His glory, we need this reflection of His glory in our lives.

I have been helped and blessed by being in the presence of some who maintained unusually deep relationships with the Lord. Also, I had the privilege of sitting under some excellent teaching ministries.

As a result of what I experienced during these times, long ago I made a very important decision. Rather than seeking after ministry, gifts, and revelation, I determined my *"first priority"* would be to seek a closer *"personal relationship"* with the Lord.

I have come to understand that as I spend quality time in the presence of God Himself, there will come into my life everything else that I have need of to fulfill His call – the anointing and quality of spirit, from which ministry, gifts, and revelation will flow.

My decision came from a life-changing experience. I attended a meeting in which the speaker gave an excellent word. He had an anointing and was reflecting light from his life, yet there was something missing.

As I left, I asked, "Lord, what is wrong? He was a great speaker, with a good word." Then the Lord brought something to my mind that John Wright Follette had said; "There is a difference between having truth itself deposited within our heart and made a part of our life, and simply reflecting truth that has come from another person or ministry."

Then I remembered another minister I had heard just a few weeks prior. I had the privilege of sitting under the ministry of the one from whom this speaker, who had left me empty, had received his ministry.

There was something in the other minister's life and ministry that made me just want to sit by her. I did not care whether she talked to me or not, because there was such a presence of God in her; I just wanted to be near to her. There was a "little open heaven" right over her head, and I felt that if only I could get close enough, I would be under it also.

Then the Lord showed me that what the second minister had ministered was good; and although there was a reflection of truth coming from his life, *the truth Himself*, the Lord Jesus Christ, had not been deposited within his life in the same way that it had been in the first minister's life.

Though very gifted and a good speaker, there was nothing that caused me to desire to linger in that speaker's presence. Suddenly my eyes opened, and I understood what the Lord was showing me.

As we are blessed by other ministries and their teachings, we must make a personal decision: Do we simply want to reflect the light that is being reflected to us, or do we want to develop within us, the relationship, from which this revelation came?

I greatly desire the relationship. Though it was many years ago that the Lord showed me this, I remember it like it was yesterday, and my decision to make my personal relationship with the Lord my first priority, has never wavered.

Each one of us needs to receive a "revelation of the relationship" that is available to us and the necessity of spending quality time alone with the Lord, that His glory might be reflected in our lives.

We cannot realize all that is attainable until we become willing to go after it.

> *"But as it is written, Eye hath not seen, nor ear heard, neither have entered into the heart of man, the things which God hath prepared for them that love him. But God hath revealed them unto us by his Spirit: for the Spirit searcheth all things, yea, the deep things of God.*

For what man knoweth the things of a man, save the spirit of man which is in him? Even so the things of God knoweth no man, but the Spirit of God. Now we have received, not the spirit of the world, but the spirit which is of God; that we might know the things that are freely given to us of God." 1 Corinthians 2:9-12

We are to seek God first and foremost for Himself. He is the foundation of everything that we need. We are to focus our seeking upon the Giver rather than upon the gift; upon the Imparter rather than upon the impartation.

The Lord desires to do a total work within each of our lives. He desires to bring forth the "Fruit of the Spirit" from within each of us. As the spiritual gifts which we have received develop, there is to come forth a greater impartation through their functioning.

Our entire lives are to become a testimony to Him, not just through our words, but through His presence in us. This will be the result of the *"Habitation of God"* being established within our being.

There is a place by God Himself that has been prepared for those who will "*turn aside*" to wait upon Him.

The Lord is looking for a people who are willing to set aside quality time to "*come apart*" to commune with Him, that He might fellowship with them. A people who will hear His call for Holiness, and live a consecrated life.

Are we willing to "come apart" and seek the Lord for Himself? There is a little chorus that I love to sing:

"For I was born to be Thy dwelling place,

A home for the presence of the Lord;

So let my life now be separated Lord to Thee,

That I might be what I was born to be."

What is your first priority?

With All My Heart

"And thou shalt love the Lord thy God with all thy heart, and with all thy soul, and with all thy mind, and with all thy strength: this is the first commandment." Mark 12:30

There is a call of God on our lives and an intimacy of relationship that is available. As we look at these scriptures may we keep in mind how much God loves those who love Him; that He is found by those who seek Him.

It is important that we are sensitive and responsive to the presence of the Lord, that we might know truth, and also be led by His spirit. Today I'd like to pray that if there be any hindrance to this in our lives, the Lord would so work in us, that it would be removed.

Rev. Hattie Hammond was in her eighties when I was privileged to have several very special visits with her. Through that personal contact, she impacted my life in a profound way. I saw in her such love for Jesus, and there was such a presence of God within her, that it stirred a hunger in me for more of the Lord. I wanted to have that kind of relationship with the Lord, too.

A process, which John Wright Follette refers to as "divine displacement," began to take place in my life, as my love for the Lord became sufficient enough to allow the cancellation of my self-life.

I once heard Hattie Hammond say as she was teaching, "Do you know where God is dealing with you? You better!" She continued, "I know where God is dealing with me! None of us are perfect; if we were, we wouldn't still be here, God would have taken us home."

A scripture that the Lord brought to life in me years ago is 2 Chronicles 15:12-15.

> "And they entered into a covenant to seek the LORD God of their fathers with all their heart and with all their soul;
>
> That whosoever would not seek the LORD God of Israel should be put to death, whether

small or great ... for they had sworn with all their heart, and sought him with their whole desire; and he was found of them: and the LORD gave them rest round about."

For several months, as I read this scripture I would express my desire to seek the Lord with all my heart, and to put to death anything within me that did not seek Him, whether it seemed big or small.

It was while I was actively praying this in private that I visited a small meeting at a barber shop. Someone spoke over my life in such a way that it seemed a direct answer to my prayer, so much so that I marked the date in my Bible by 2 Chronicles 15:15 as a word from the Lord to me.

Below are some other scriptures that have gone deep into my spirit through prayer as well:

"Search me, O God, and know my heart: try me, and know my thoughts: And see if there be any wicked way in me, and lead me in the way everlasting." Psalm 139:23-24

"Create in me a clean heart, O God; and renew a right spirit within me." Psalm 51:10

"Who can understand his errors? Cleanse thou me from secret faults. Keep back thy servant also from presumptuous sins; let them not have dominion over me..." Psalm 19:12-13

"For I will declare mine iniquity; I will be sorry for my sin." Psalm 38:18

Song of Solomon 2:15, speaks of *"little foxes, that spoil the vines."* How important it is that we allow the Holy Spirit to search and cleanse our hearts.

These are scriptures we can hold in our hearts before the Lord that they might set the poise of our spirit, creating a door for the Lord to walk through as we spend time in His presence. May the Lord work these attitudes deep into our spirits, that our hearts might always be soft and tender towards Him.

Levels of Spiritual Growth

"But grow in grace, and in the knowledge of our Lord and Saviour Jesus Christ. To him be glory both now and forever. Amen." 2 Peter 3:18

Ephesians 2:8-9 tells us:

"For by grace are you saved through faith; and that not of yourselves: it is the gift of God: Not of works, lest any man should boast."

Salvation is through faith in the Lord Jesus Christ. We realize that we have all sinned, coming short of the glory of God in our lives (Romans 3:23). But if we confess our sins, God is faithful and just to forgive us and cleanse us from all unrighteousness (John 1:9).

Through faith in the shed blood of the Lord Jesus Christ we are reconciled, or brought back into right relationship with God.

"Therefore being justified by faith, we have peace with God through our Lord Jesus Christ." Romans 5:1

This is the greatness of God's love toward us!

"But after that the kindness and love of God our Saviour toward man appeared, Not by works of righteousness which we have done, but according to his mercy he saved us, by the washing of regeneration, and renewing of the Holy Ghost;

Which he shed on us abundantly through Jesus Christ our Saviour; That being justified by His grace, we should be made heirs according to the hope of eternal life." Titus 3:4-7

Works, or what we do, are important, not as a means of salvation but as evidence of our faith. Faith, if it does not have works is dead, being alone (James 2:17).

By works, or as we live out what we say we believe, our faith is made perfect, or comes to maturity (James

2:22). James speaks of faith and actions working together that faith might be made complete by the choices we make and the things we do.

Choices! We all make them, every day of our lives. It is through these choices that our faith grows and comes to maturity, as it is being worked out in our everyday life. Character, or who I am, is a result of choices I have made day after day, year after year.

As I come to know the Lord and receive His grace into my life, I begin to choose the Lord and His ways. As I do, His nature and character is formed in me. I am brought into the position where I can say *"it is no longer I, but Christ that dwells in me"* (Galatians 2:20).

The parable below speaks of those who bear fruit, thirty, sixty or one hundred fold.

> *"But he that received seed into the good ground is he that hears the word, and understands it; which also bears fruit, and brings forth, some an hundredfold, some sixty, some thirty."* Matthew 13:23

The seed falling on the wayside speaks of those who have no spiritual understanding. They hear the Word, but it does not impact their life in any way.

Stony ground speaks of those who hear the Word with joy, but there is no depth in their life. They allow offences to harbor in their heart. Rather than dealing with problems rightly, their ground becomes stony, hindering the seed from coming forth.

Thorny ground speaks of those who hear the Word, but they are just too busy to cultivate a spiritual walk and relationship with the Lord. The cares of this life and the desire for the things of this world fill up their calendar, and the seed they have received gets choked out with the busyness of a carnal life.

Each of these types of soil are in the garden of our own lives. Yet we can recognize this and begin to garden with tender care, that the seed can come forth in its fullest potential.

I can recognize my need for greater spiritual understanding, and begin to pray like Paul, for the

Spirit which is from God that I might know and understand spiritual things (1 Corinthians 2:12).

I can deal with offences as they come into my life, allowing God to work in me and change me as I forgive (Matthew 6:12).

I can make time for the Lord in my own personal prayer closet as well as in gathering with other Christians, as the Word instructs me to do (Matthew 6:6; Hebrews 10:25).

I can seek first to please the Lord in all I do (Matthew 6:33). Through my attitudes and actions, the Lord can become my first priority in life (Psalm 27:4).

Choices and priorities! We all have them. I am saved by grace, but I grow through the choices I make.

Philippians tells us that we are to *"work out our own salvation with fear and trembling, for it is God who works in us to will and to do His good pleasure"* (Philippians 2:12-13).

Through choices the very nature of the Lord Jesus Christ is being formed in me, thirty fold, sixty fold, one hundred fold, depending on my yieldedness to the working of the Lord within and my willingness to cultivate the soil of my life.

As I yield to the Lord, through time, I will grow. We may not always realize it, but change is taking place in our lives. It is like a child – you do not realize he has grown until you try to put a piece of clothing on him he has not worn for awhile. It does not fit!

> *"And he said, So is the kingdom of God, as if a man should cast seed into the ground; And should sleep, and rise night and day, and the seed should spring and grow up, he knows not how.*
>
> *For the earth brings forth fruit of herself; first the blade, then the ear, after that the full corn in the ear."* Mark 4:26-28

Spiritual maturity takes time. I may not feel like I have much. But though the seed that I have received into my life may be as the least of all seeds, when it is grown it becomes a mighty tree, where others can come and find refreshment from the Christ in me.

"Another parable put he forth unto them, saying, The kingdom of heaven is like to a grain of mustard seed, which a man took, and sowed in his field:

Which indeed is the least of all seeds: but when it is grown, it is the greatest among herbs, and becomes a tree, so that the birds of the air come and lodge in the branches thereof." Matthew 13:31–32

Something Walter Beuttler once said has had a great impact on my life. "If we will build the Lord a house of devotion, He will build us a house of ministry."

If we can keep our focus on the *"coming"* and *"being"* rather than being distracted by the *"going"* and *"doing,"* the reproduction of Christ within our own lives will bring forth the true life and ministry of Christ; the Holy Spirit first changing us, then flowing through us to touch others. This is the transforming power and presence of God we so desperately need in our midst today!

Key to our spiritual growth is spiritual hunger. Through the regeneration of the Holy Spirit, we have been given hunger as part of our new birth experience. That hunger is a gift from God.

A baby is created with hunger because without that hunger the baby would not eat. Food is necessary for life. It is up to us to nurture the hunger God has given us, developing an appetite pleasing to the Lord and conducive to our spiritual growth, that we might continue to grow in an experiential knowledge of God.

2 Thessalonians 1:10 speaks of the Lord coming to be glorified in His saints and to be admired in all them that believe. What a glorious calling! That Jesus would be seen and admired in me, in you! In every circumstance, in every place, that we can be a witness to Him (Acts 1:8).

> *"Wherefore also we pray always for you, that our God would count you worthy of this calling, and fulfill all the good pleasure of His goodness, and the work of faith with power:*

That the name of our Lord Jesus Christ may be glorified in you, and you in Him, according to the grace of our God and the Lord Jesus Christ." 2 Thessalonians 1:11–12

May we make right choices! And maintain the soil of our lives carefully. Walking worthy of His calling.

That I May Know Him

"That I may know him, and the power of his resurrection, and the fellowship of his sufferings, being made conformable to his death." Philippians 3:10

Due to the call of God on my dad's life, I grew up on Bible school campuses. Though only a child, I was blessed to know the students and to participate in some of their activities.

One particular school encouraged the memorization of scripture during our free time. Then at supper, table by table, we would go around the room competitively quoting from the book of Philippians. How wonderful to memorize scripture! I have always wondered if this is why I love the book of Philippians so much even today.

Paul's letter to the Philippian church simply expresses his own desire for the Lord. His letter is not long, only about four pages in most Bibles. Even so, Paul writes so personally, that the first-person pronoun "I" is used at least one hundred times.

Not composed as a defense or to correct problems in the church, Paul conveys his own desire for the Lord and also encourages the Philippian church in their walk and relationship with the Lord.

What is the cry of Paul's heart? Let's contemplate this: Paul was an apostle. He had a powerful conversion experience on the road to Damascus. He was caught up into the heavenlies where he saw things beyond expression.

Yet, listen to his cry in Philippians 3:10: *"That I may know Him, and the power of His resurrection, and the fellowship of His sufferings, being made conformable to His death."*

Years ago, there was a man in our church who would often sing the song, "Lord, I Want to Know You More." Tears would run down his face as he sang not just with his voice, but with his heart.

Each time he sang, our hearts would be moved. He could not sing that song enough because, each time, it was a fresh cry coming from his own hunger for more of the Lord. As the Lord responded to his cry, we all would be brought into a deeper presence of the Lord as our own hearts were being stirred for yet more of the Lord.

Such was the cry in Paul's heart to know the Lord. Paul said, *"If by any means I might attain unto the resurrection of the dead"* (Philippians 3:11). Paul wasn't worried about not being saved or losing his salvation. Looking at this verse in the Greek you will see it means, *"If by any means I might attain unto an out resurrection from among the living dead."*

Paul's burning desire was to be lifted out from mere religious form into a living fellowship and identification with the Lord Jesus Christ. This inner desire for more of the Lord can never be satisfied through learning just facts or information about God. Nor can it be satisfied through religious ritual void of the presence of God.

We were created for fellowship with a living God. Through a growing, personal relationship with Him, I can gain knowledge of His heart and thoughts as I come to know His person; who He is.

Daily, as I learn to discern His presence, I come to know what pleases the Lord and what grieves His Holy Spirit. As I identify with His heart and open myself to His inner working, I start to become more like Him. A greater understanding of the Lord is formed in me, as every part of who I am is brought into greater unity with who He is.

> *"Not as though I had already attained, either were already perfect: but I follow after, if that I may apprehend that for which also I am apprehended of Christ Jesus."* Philippians 3:12

As with any relationship, knowing the Lord and becoming one with Him will increase over time as we maintain our poise of spirit toward Him.

Through this increasing oneness of spirit, as we are brought into an identification with the Lord and His heart; we come into alignment not only with who He is, but with what He is doing. This opens the door for His purpose to be fulfilled in our lives in a greater way, that we might apprehend that for which we have been apprehended.

What is God's will for our lives? First and foremost, it is that we would know Him. This is what salvation is all about! Not just a membership into heaven, but a growing relationship with our Lord and Saviour, Jesus Christ. Notice the wording in these verses:

> *"And he goeth up into a mountain, and calleth unto him whom he would: and they came unto him.*
>
> *And he ordained twelve, that they should be with him, and that he might send them forth to preach, And to have power to heal sicknesses, and to cast out devils."* Mark 3:13-15

He went *"up."* The call of God is always to come up into a higher dimension of living and relationship with

Him. Then, He called whom He would. Why? That they might be with Him!

Because of their time with Him, when He sent them, they went in His power, with His heart and His way of thinking, as a witness or expression of Himself.

We must *"come"* before we can *"do."* So often our eyes catch the *doing*, without noticing the *coming*. It is from the *coming* that we can then *do*. He is the vine, we are the branches. Without Him we can *do* nothing! As my dad used to say, "Two times nothing is nothing!" We can't give what we don't have!

Once, someone asked me why a particular person had said something. I did not know, nor had I even known they had said it. But I had spent a lot of time with that person; I understood their way of thinking. So, I replied that if they had said that, it was probably because of reasons that I then explained.

Later, I checked with that person to see if I was right. Absolutely! How did I know? From having spent time in their presence and coming to know them, their heart, their way of thinking.

My son, now an adult, was a beautiful baby. I could not have loved him more when he was first born. I adored him! Yet, as he grew and became a man, there came a fellowship that we now can have, a functioning together, that we never could have had if he had stayed in his original infant state.

Salvation is the first step of a beautiful, new relationship with the Lord Jesus Christ. Then, it is the Lord's desire that we *"grow in grace, and in the knowledge of our Lord and Saviour Jesus Christ"* (2 Peter 3:18a).

The Lord is longing for us to grow up into Him, that we might become a part of who He is, a sample of Him in the earth today. We are called to *be* a witness, not to *do* witnessing (Acts 1:8). So often we see the *do* and fall short of the *being*. From the *being*, will come a *doing*, but *doing* alone falls short of the call of God on our lives.

> *"To whom God would make known what is the riches of the glory of this mystery among*

the Gentiles; which is Christ in you, the hope of glory." Colossians 1:27

Through an increasing oneness of spirit and identity with the Lord's heart, may we come into alignment with who He is and what He is doing, that His purpose be fulfilled in our lives in a greater way.

A scripture I have prayed for years, "Lord, cause me to apprehend that for which I have been apprehended." May this be your prayer too.

Section 3
Working of God Within

The Blessedness of Right Relationship with God

In Psalm 32, David writes about a time of conviction and the chastening of the Lord in his life. He confesses his sin and tells of the Lord's faithfulness to forgive him. David then goes on to speak of the blessedness of being in right relationship with the Lord.

> "Blessed is he whose transgression is forgiven, whose sin is covered." Psalm 32:1

> "Blessed is the man unto whom the LORD imputeth not iniquity, and in whose spirit

there is no guile." Psalm 32:2

There are times when God deals with us until we come to a place of repentance:

"When I kept silence, my bones waxed old through my roaring all the day long." Psalm 32:3

"For day and night thy hand was heavy upon me: my moisture is turned into the drought of summer. Selah." Psalm 32:4

Once we acknowledge our sin, the Lord is faithful to forgive us:

"I acknowledged my sin unto thee, and mine iniquity have I not hid. I said, I will confess my transgressions unto the LORD; and thou forgavest the iniquity of my sin. Selah." Psalm 32:5

There is a blessing that rests on those who are in right relationship with God:

"For this shall every one that is godly pray

unto thee in a time when thou mayest be found: surely in the floods of great waters they shall not come nigh unto him." Psalm 32:6

The godly call on the Lord and find protection even in overwhelming circumstances. There is a place of rest and safety in the presence of the Lord:

"Thou art my hiding place; thou shalt preserve me from trouble; thou shalt compass me about with songs of deliverance. Selah." Psalm 32:7

The Lord promises to lead and guide those who have a right relationship with Him as they look to Him:

"I will instruct thee and teach thee in the way which thou shalt go: I will guide thee with mine eye." Psalm 32:8

Then the Psalmist admonishes us:

"Be ye not as the horse, or as the mule, which have no understanding: whose mouth must be held in with bit and bridle, lest they come

near unto thee." Psalm 32:9

He points out the contrast of those who don't and those who do put their trust in the Lord:

"Many sorrows shall be to the wicked: but he that trusteth in the LORD, mercy shall compass him about." Psalm 32:10

He then expresses his joy at being forgiven, and the joy of all those who are upright:

"Be glad in the LORD, and rejoice, ye righteous: and shout for joy, all ye that are upright in heart." Psalm 32:11

These, simply written, are keys to living in right relationship with God. How we need this level of repentance, relationship, perception, and blessing in our lives!

I have laid this out using the King James Bible; you may want to read Psalm 32 in several other translations as well, to help you gain a deeper appreciation of what David has written.

From a place of love, devotion, and obedience we can live our lives in right relationship to God and know the blessings that follow.

We need to be fine-tuned to the Lord, to know His thoughts, to know His ways, and to be directed by His Holy Spirit. I can testify of times when that gentle inner nudge of the Holy Spirit has made a huge difference in my life. This is so important in the times we are living in today!

May we adjust our activities to make room for more focused time in the Lord's presence. May times of worship resonate in our hearts. May we meditate on God's Word. May we be drawn ever closer to Him.

My prayer for you is that the Lord ever lead and guide you. That He bless you in every way. That He provide for your every need. That you are drawn ever closer to Him.

For those who need comfort, that God will comfort. For those who need direction, that the Lord will direct. Whatever the need, that you will turn to the Lord

Jesus Christ and find the strength, wisdom, and peace He has for you.

May we be a godly example to others, a place where people can sense His peace, His presence, and His life in us, that they also might be encouraged to experience the blessedness of having a right relationship with God.

The Upward Call

"Christ in you, the hope of glory." Colossians 1:27b

Some words a friend, Janice Huse, wrote: "O Lord my heart longs to be, a habitation fit for Thee, a place where peace reigns, and love can flourish, a heart where You will feel at home."

Does the Lord feel at home in our hearts? Do our attitudes and thoughts make a comfortable atmosphere for Him to abide in?

Some time ago I was dealing with dynamics that caused everything within me to want to react. Then I remembered a situation in my dad's life. A quote from his book, *The Secret of the Stairs*:

"As I stood in the freezing rain upon that pile of unloaded lumber, an intense warfare raged within me. Then a verse from Job came to me, 'though He slay me, yet will I trust Him' (Job 13:15a), and I began to melt. I repeated this to the Lord and said, 'Lord, I do not care what happens to me, I am going all the way with You.'

Just then, something of eternal value and substance was created deep within my being. I was changed. A deep inner peace, along with an imparted ability to obey the Lord, developed within me, and I was able to finish unloading the truck. My commitment to the Lord was literally burned into the fiber of my being through the intensity of this situation."

As I remembered my dad's experience, suddenly I saw not the circumstance but the Lord working in me. What a victory as I yielded to the Lord that day!

I am so thankful for the working of the Lord in our lives! This inner working of the Holy Spirit deep inside us is what brings us into a true fellowship with Him and with each other.

> *"But if we walk in the light, as he is in the light, we have fellowship one with another, and the blood of Jesus Christ his Son cleanses us from all sin."* 1 John 1:7

"For we are his workmanship, created in Christ Jesus unto good works, which God hath before ordained that we should walk in them." Ephesians 2:10

"And he that searcheth the hearts knoweth what is the mind of the Spirit, because he maketh intercession for the saints according to the will of God. And we know that all things work together for good to them that love God, to them who are the called according to his purpose." Romans 8:27–28

Years ago, I did not notice the word *"and"* between verses 27 and 28 in Romans 8. There is intercession taking place for you and for me, even now. As we yield to the Holy Spirit, a working of the Lord takes place, His workmanship, that all things might "work together for good" in our hearts and lives.

What is that good? That good is Christ being formed in us.

"For whom he did foreknow, he also did predestinate to be conformed to the image

of his Son, that he might be the firstborn among many brethren." Romans 8:29

We are called to be partakers of His divine nature (2 Peter 1:4). *"Christ in you, the hope of glory"* (Colossians 1:27b). That *"as he is, so are we in this world"* (1 John 4:17b).

We must be born again (John 3:7). We are saved through faith; salvation is a gift from God, *"not of works lest any man should boast"* (Ephesians 2:9).

But then the Word says if any man would follow after the Lord, he is to deny himself and take up his cross and follow after Him (Matthew 16:24). Luke makes it clear we are to do this daily (Luke 9:23). The apostle Paul said in 1 Corinthians 15:31 that he died daily!

Choice! There is a working of the Lord within that which we "should" and, if we are wise, "will" yield to. The Holy Spirit makes intercession for us, that this good can come forth in our lives.

There is an upward call within the church, that we might become that dwelling place for the presence of the Lord. That His shadow might cover us. That His glory might be seen. That we might become a conduit for His presence, impacting the earth today.

This is the secret of the stairs! That I meet the Lord in the circumstance that I am in. Then that becomes the platform for me to meet the Lord again. Difficulty becomes a riser in my walk and relationship with Him, bringing me up to the next platform upon which I can then make another right choice.

As I follow on to know the Lord, that pattern repeats itself as I am lifted up into His presence, a place of intimacy with Him where time and time again I can surrender to the Lord, allowing Him to work within my heart. What a glorious calling!

When we know how to respond rightly, trouble becomes but a servant, an opportunity for God to do a further work in our lives. When we see this, we will become that habitation, a place where peace reigns and love can flourish. A heart where God will feel at home. Perhaps you will join me as I say, "This is my desire! Lord, let it be…"

A Yielded Heart

"Who is this that cometh up from the wilderness, leaning upon her beloved?"
Song of Solomon 8:5

The passion of my heart is to be able to say, *"Yes, Lord,"* regardless of the situation, circumstance, or challenge. It is essential to recognize and yield to the *workmanship* of God within if we are to grow in our walk with the Lord. A deeper relationship with the Lord is available, but it requires a trust and submission to the Lord in the daily circumstances of our lives.

Walking in a place of submission involves receiving our calling and the understanding that He has given us, then not becoming possessive of it, but saying, "Lord, I submit all of this back to You." The door will then open for us to hear more and be led further.

Abraham knew that he had heard from God. He had been told to take his son, Isaac, up the mount and sacrifice him. If Abraham had not been open to hearing further, he may not have noticed the lamb in the thicket that the Lord provided as a substitute sacrifice. Abraham's attitude of *submissive dependence* enabled him to enter the fullness of the Lord's plan, which he understood only in part at that time.

Jesus is the potter, and we are the clay. We are in the process of becoming that which He sees us to be. He is all-knowing; He knows the end from the beginning. Therefore, we must trust Him fully, regardless of what our perception or thought might be at any particular moment in our lives.

There have been many times of "adjustment" in my own life. During these times, I have been encouraged as I remember some of my dad's experiences.

At times when the Lord spoke, my dad thought he knew what would happen, and when it didn't come to pass, he could be disappointed at the moment; but down the road, when things had turned out to be quite different, he always rejoiced because he realized what the Lord had intended was much better than anything he initially expected.

A *teachable* spirit that loves the Lord and continues to trust and submit, will bring us through to the full intention and purpose of our Lord — His highest and best in our lives. We must always maintain a stance of submission to the Lord, knowing that we need the continued leading and guidance of His Holy Spirit.

The Song of Solomon is a story of submission. There is an awakening to the love song of the Lord that brings an *initial hunger* for Him. From that initial hunger comes a *continued* hunger, which opens the door for the inward working of the Lord.

The bride does not turn aside from seeking the one she loves (Jesus), regardless of any difficulty she faces or solace offered by others. Because of her continued poise of spirit toward the Lord, she finds Him.

"It was but a little that I passed from them, but I found him whom my soul loveth: I held him, and would not let him go..." Song of Solomon 3:4

Through all that she experienced, as she continued to seek her heavenly Bridegroom, the bride was brought into a place of desire for Him alone and, as a result, found her place of participation with Him in His purposes.

"I am my beloved's, and his desire is toward me. Come, my beloved, let us go forth into the field..." Song of Solomon 7:10-11

The Lord is calling us today into this same place of intimacy, submission, and participation with Him.

"Behold, I stand at the door, and knock: if any man hear my voice, and open the door, I will come in to him, and will sup with him, and he with me." Revelation 3:20

After we "hear the voice of the Lord" and "open the door," we are enabled to hear the "sound of the trumpet" that leads to a revelation of the One sitting on the Throne, and the unfolding of things to come:

> *"After this I looked, and, behold, a door was opened in heaven: and the first voice which I heard was as it were of a trumpet talking with me; which said, Come up hither, and I will show thee things which must be hereafter.*
>
> *And immediately I was in the spirit: and, behold, a throne was set in heaven, and one sat on the throne."* Revelation 4:1-2

The desire of the Lord is toward those who desire Him. There is much emphasis today on *doing*, but there is a longing in the heart of the Lord for those who yearn to *become* that which He would have them to be. While there *is* an outward expression, it must spring from the touch of His presence within us.

There are *situations* that the Lord uses as *tools* to work His image and likeness into our being. The very service or ministry into which the Lord is calling us, may be an *instrument* to change us. God may be using our availability to do something *through* us, but He also desires to do a further work *in* us!

Like Paul, I am to press toward the mark for the prize — the fullness of God in my life. As Charles Haun taught, "We will go as far as our surrender will take us. We will be filled with as much as we can empty."

There are times when we are given assignments where we try to be "strong for Jesus." Even in these areas, there is a submission to the Lord that allows His working within and the intervention of God on our behalf.

Kathryn Kuhlman would ask the Lord if she had been more *yielded*, would one more person have been healed? The key to the power in her ministry was *knowing* and *yielding* to the Holy Spirit; not becoming strong, but *submitted* and *yielded*.

The Lord worked within Kathryn's heart a great love and compassion for people. She said if ever she had lost that love, she never would have spoken another message again.

Rees Howell went through tremendous dealings in his life that brought him into a deeper place of *yieldedness* to the Lord.

From this position of *yieldedness*, and through intercession and prayer, the Lord was able to use him and those who were joined together with him to intervene even in international events. He learned to *yield to* and follow the leading of the Holy Spirit, allowing the Holy Spirit to move through him.

The Lord is calling each of us into a place of intimacy and participation with Him. It is a place of *yieldedness* and submission, a place of hearing and being led by the Holy Spirit, that we might become united with Him.

"I am my beloved's, and his desire is toward me. Come, my beloved, let us go forth into the field ... there will I give thee my loves." Song of Solomon 7:10-12

My prayer is for an increase of the inner working of the Lord within each of our lives. It may not always feel good, and we may not always like or seemingly appreciate it, but in time, we will recognize that His inner workings are intended to bring us to His highest and best.

Years ago, a person had seen something with the words, "Yes, Lord," and told John Wright Follette that when they saw those words, they were reminded of him.

Many years later, someone who heard this story, engraved those same words on a wood plaque and gave it to my dad. They said that when they heard that story, it made them think of him. Today I have that little plaque hanging on my wall. It is one of my most treasured possessions.

Lord, may this be the mark of my life, and others —
simply, "Yes, Lord."

Birthed in Brokenness

"My heart rejoiceth in the Lord, mine horn is exalted in the Lord; my mouth is enlarged over mine enemies; because I rejoice in thy salvation. There is none holy as the Lord, for there is none beside Thee; neither is there any rock like our God." 1 Samuel 2:1-2

The name of Hannah's antagonist, "Peninnah," fittingly means "pearl." Pearls form as a result of the discomfort caused by an agitating grain of sand lodged within a mollusk.

Hannah was barren, which was a reproach in that day. Peninnah had children, and each year as they went to the temple to offer their sacrifice, she would provoke Hannah, causing her to weep.

It appeared that Peninnah was favored due to her children. But Hannah, although barren, was greatly beloved. As she wept, her husband would express his love for her, but human comfort could not satisfy the cry that was within Hannah's heart.

Little did Hannah understand as she wept day after day, that this all was part of God's plan! How often the Lord uses less than perfect circumstances in our own lives, when we yield to Him, not only to work in us for our own benefit, but also as preparation for a much higher purpose.

> *"And we know that all things work together for good to them that love God, to them who are the called according to his purpose.*
>
> *For whom he did foreknow, he also did predestinate to be conformed to the image of his Son, that he might be the firstborn among many brethren."* Romans 8:28-29

In order to birth the prophetic voice that the Lord desired at that time, it was necessary for Hannah to enter into a state of brokenness. Although she was seeing only her present personal situation in the moment, there was a bigger picture that pertained to the Lord's people and His purposes.

Hannah may have been content to remain barren were it not for an adversary in her life who provoked her, causing her to cry out to the Lord for a son. As pressures worked to intensify that desire within Hannah, God heard her cry, and in this state of brokenness, Hannah brought forth a man child who became the prophetic voice that was needed in that day.

> *"For this child I prayed; and the LORD hath given me my petition which I asked of him."* 1 Samuel 1:27

> *"And Samuel grew, and the LORD was with him, and did let none of his words fall to the ground."* 1 Samuel 3:19

It was a time of transition. Eli, the high priest, was aware that his heritage would be displaced, because the Lord had sent a prophet to pronounce judgment upon his household. Even so, when Hannah brought Samuel into the temple, Eli received and nurtured him.

If Eli's heart had been hardened as was Saul's, he would have risen up against Samuel like Saul trying to kill David. But Eli did not do this; rather, he valued the things of God and held in high regard the word of the Lord.

Nonetheless, the vision of Eli had grown dim. There was no "present word" from the Lord. Though he knew his sons were doing evil, he did not restrain them. Although Eli loved the Lord, he had become fat; that is, he had allowed compromise in his life and ministry.

The child, Samuel, was given not only to lift the reproach from Hannah, but for God's higher purpose in birthing the prophetic voice needed at that particular time. For that voice to come forth in power, that which was birthed had to be fully consecrated and given to the Lord. The pressure Hannah experienced worked to bring a brokenness of spirit within her, causing her to make this necessary consecration within her life.

There is a barrenness today that many are recognizing, and it is producing an inner cry. The "Peninnahs" of our day are causing this cry to increase. There are always those who do not understand the depth of this cry when it comes.

As it begins to surface, there are those who will wonder what is wrong with us or pat us on the back and say, "cheer up." Eli saw Hannah's lips moving in prayer, but did not understand why — he thought she was drunk!

Just as Hannah would not allow herself to be comforted by the kind words of others, so there is a need today for those who will never become satisfied with just gifts or provisions given to make them comfortable. For those who have this deep inner cry, it is important they do not allow themselves to be satisfied with any consolation less than the Lord Himself. The Word tells us that Hannah continued in prayer before the Lord until He spoke.

As she persevered, there grew within Hannah the willingness to fully consecrate to the Lord the man child she so desperately desired. This released the Lord to speak a word through Eli that a child would be given to her. Once Hannah received this assurance, she wept no more. Soon after, Samuel was conceived. Now, Hannah's tears became a song:

> *"My heart rejoiceth in the LORD, mine horn is exalted in the LORD; my mouth is enlarged over mine enemies; because I rejoice in thy salvation. There is none holy as the LORD, for there is none beside thee; neither is there any rock like our God."* 1 Samuel 2:1-2

I had considered this song to be Hannah's rejoicing over her adversary because she now had a child and was no longer barren. But this song of rejoicing goes much deeper than that. It did not come forth after the birth of Samuel, but only after he had been weaned and fully consecrated to the Lord.

The exultation in Hannah's heart was not over this woman who had provoked her, nor was it mere triumph because her state of barrenness had been broken. She triumphed in being able to deliver this child to the Lord as she had petitioned.

Hannah had not only birthed Samuel, but she had fulfilled her vow before the Lord. This was a great victory within her own life. She had a son in the temple. Others did not know, nor did they need to know; she knew that the Lord had given this child to her and that she had fulfilled her vow by giving him back to the Lord.

The Lord is looking for "Hannahs" in this day and hour. There is coming forth the Kingdom rule of God in and through a people who are to rule with a rod of iron.

But this end-time prophetic voice must first be birthed in a state of brokenness, bringing an inner submission to the Lord Jesus Christ. The birth pangs are a deep inner cry within a heart that can be satisfied with nothing less than a present word from the Lord.

"Thou hast enlarged me when I was in distress..." Psalm 4:1

This level of inner brokenness brings a yieldedness to the Lord. The Scriptures say of the child that Hannah brought forth, "none of his words fell to the ground." His voice was used solely for the purposes of the Lord.

Because of the depth of consecration, submission and yieldedness within, God was able to bring forth a prophetic voice accompanied with a God-given authority.

> *"And he that overcometh, and keepeth my works unto the end, to him will I give power over the nations: And he shall rule them with a rod of iron."* Revelation 2:26-27a

We said that the name "Peninnah" means "pearl." This reveals to us that Hannah's trouble had been pre-arranged by the Lord to be used as her servant, the very thing necessary to bring forth the purpose of God in her life. The antagonist that troubled Hannah was actually serving her. The agitation caused by Peninnah produced the pearl that became Samuel, the prophet.

If this woman had not provoked her, Hannah might have been content in her relationship with her husband and the gifts he gave her. She needed this pressure in order to come into that which the Lord desired for her.

It is very important during our times of trouble that we are careful in how we respond or react. When we are under pressure, we usually try to rearrange our circumstances or make adjustments so we will feel a little better. But the Lord is seeking to do something closer to us than we may realize.

"Blessed are the poor in spirit: for theirs is the kingdom of heaven." Matthew 5:3

As we are willing to break before the Lord, yielding to Him, He will be able to bring forth that which He intends. We will see the rule of Christ come forth through a corporate people who have allowed this deep inner working of the Lord in their hearts, because they are confident that:

"We are his workmanship, created in Christ Jesus unto good works, which God hath before ordained that we should walk in them." Ephesians 2:10

"For it is God which worketh in you both to will and to do of his good pleasure." Philippians 2:13

"Being confident of this very thing, that he which hath begun a good work in you will perform it until the day of Jesus Christ."
Philippians 1:6

May we be confident of that which the Lord is doing not only in our lives, but in the times we are in. Let us look not at the "Peninnahs" He has allowed, but at the man child coming forth through a broken, yet victorious people who have set their face toward the Lord and will settle for nothing less than His intervention.

****

Lord, in the "pearls" we face, may we see a greater purpose fulfilled, as You bring us from brokenness into victory.

Section 4
Inner Change

Inner Transformation

"For it is God which worketh in you both to will and to do of his good pleasure."
Philippians 2:13

Years ago, my dad had an aloe plant in his office. One day he broke off a piece to rub some of the gel on his finger, and then discarded it. He told it like this: "The aloe plant called out from the trash can and said, 'Is this the way you treat me after I gave my life so you could have healing? You use me and then throw me in the trash can?'"

How much easier it is to give when we can expect some gain in return, or at least appreciation. But Jesus said of Himself, *"For even the Son of man came not to be ministered unto, but to minister, and to give his life a ransom for many"* (Mark 10:45).

When the early church gave recognition to those from whom they could expect a favor, James rebuked them, telling them neither their hearts nor their motives were pure. In fact, he said it very strongly:

> *"If you really fulfill the royal law according to the Scripture, 'You shall love your neighbor as yourself,' you do well; but if you show partiality, you commit sin, and are convicted by the law as transgressors."* James 2:8-9 NKJV

Inner drives, inner needs, practical needs ... so many things can motivate us, often without us even being aware. But then something will come along and expose our hearts. We may feel a lack of regard or appreciation from others. Someone may be making demands on our time. When tempted to react, how can we turn from being like that complaining little aloe plant to being like Jesus, whose sole delight was in loving His heavenly Father and doing His will?

This transformation requires an inner working of the Lord, often through circumstances and our willingness in those circumstances to allow the Lord to work in our hearts. During such times, it can be easy to feel sorry for ourselves or seek comfort from others.

If we will, instead, submit ourselves to the Lord, He can bring an inner change, where lesser motives are put to death as His higher law of love begins to work in us — a love first toward the Lord, then reflected toward others.

As I am able to yield to the Lord during times of heat and pressure, the very fiber of who I am and how I react is dealt with, as not only my behavior changes, but His nature is formed in me.

> *"For whom the Lord loves he chastens, and scourges every son whom he receives."*
> Hebrews 12:6

Chastening corrects sin or wrong behavior. When we do wrong, the Lord will bring a correction. If we are honest, we will realize we deserve the correction, and receive it, recognizing the Lord's love.

Scourging works on a deeper level. For example, maybe we did not do wrong, but we are still being blamed. It is within our very nature to react when unfair things come against us.

As we choose to respond rightly during difficult times, something that might have made us bitter, instead becomes a tool in the Lord's hands. Not all things are good, but God promises to work all things together for good, for them that love Him (Romans 8:28).

As we allow His working in our lives, more than our outward behavior is changed. That which reacts inside of us is also dealt with, bringing us into a place beyond reaction, to responding in the nature of Christ.

> *"But now, O LORD, thou art our father; we are the clay, and thou our potter; and we all are the work of thy hand."* Isaiah 64:8

Scripture speaks of being *"more than conquerors"* through Christ Jesus and His love for us (Romans 8:37). I may go through something that touches a particular area of my inner being; I overcome by choosing to allow the Lord to work in me through that situation.

But then, the Lord allows another circumstance, again touching me deep inside, and again, I make the choice to overcome. This time, as I yield to the Lord, I come through on a higher level. I am not just going through the same reactions or the same feelings over and over. There is a progressive working of the Lord taking place in my life, where my very nature is being dealt with and I am being changed into the image of His Son.

> *"And the vessel that he made of clay was marred in the hand of the potter: so he made it again another vessel, as seemed good to the potter to make it."* Jeremiah 18:4

Why is this process so important? Jesus said, *"For the prince of this world cometh, and hath nothing in me.*

But that the world may know that I love the Father; and as the Father gave me commandment, even so I do" (John 14:30b–31).

Because Jesus was sinless and His nature perfect, even as the Son of man, no pressure was able to deviate Him from His purpose. He had no selfish motivation. Nothing caused Him to react wrongly. He fully did the will of His heavenly Father and was a complete expression of Him in the earth.

Scripture refers to Jesus as the firstborn among many brethren (Romans 8:29). As we approach the Kingdom age, the Lord is looking for those who are willing to submit to His inner working, that they might be brought into a place of total obedience to Him.

It is important that our natures have been so dealt with, that no lesser thing will move or motivate us. No selfish ambition will drive us. The will of God alone will rule us, as we give expression to Christ within.

The Lord is preparing a people today who will usher in His glory as He releases His authority in the earth in the days ahead. The testing of the faith of those He is working in is precious in His sight, as He prepares them to participate with Him in the coming days of His presence.

> *"The precious sons of Zion, comparable to fine gold, how are they esteemed as earthen pitchers, the work of the hands of the potter!"*
> Lamentations 4:2

Hebrews 11:6b tells us, *"He that cometh to God must believe that he is, and that he is a rewarder of them that diligently seek him."* John tells us, *"This is the work of God, that ye believe on him"* (John 6:29b).

As situations come our way and we maintain our awareness of the present reality of a God who is, who is working in our lives, and who loves us, then we are able to look beyond people and circumstances to the Lord, recognize His inner working, and rest in expectation of His purposes being fulfilled.

As a bride, our love is set on the Lord, and we spend time fellowshipping in His presence. But as sons, we must allow the Lord to prepare us that we might participate with Him in a greater way, as He unveils His power in the coming days.

We must realize that being shaped into true Christ-likeness will not come easily. God may use the most seemingly trivial situation to work out His greater purposes in our lives.

May we learn to be sensitive to His inner working and yield to Him, as He brings us into alignment with His higher purposes. May we be a part of that people the Lord is preparing today, a people being birthed into an active end-time relationship with Him.

Deep Inner Trust in the Lord

"I will say of the LORD, He is my refuge and my fortress: my God; in him will I trust." Psalm 91:2

I have often been challenged in my own life by the life of David, a man after God's own heart! In other words, there was something within the very fiber of David that pleased the Lord.

"I have found David the son of Jesse, a man after mine own heart, which shall fulfil all my will." Acts 13:22

Reading through the Psalms, it becomes evident that as David sought the Lord in his own life circumstances, the words that flowed from his heart moved beyond his own situations and emotions, into an identification with the Lord, as he gave prophetic expression to the very life of Christ (see Acts 2:25).

From that place of identification with the heart of God, the Lord was able to further reveal Himself through

David, as He moved to accomplish His will not only in David's life, but in a people.

Though the favor of the Lord rested on David, David's life was not always easy. He knew what it meant to be disregarded, rejected, and alone; to have others turn against him. He was a man of war, yet he had a heart of worship. There was faith in David, with tenacity to stand. Songs flowed from his harp as he played before the Lord ... songs of love, songs of trust, songs of repentance, songs of commitment. David's poise of spirit pleased the Lord.

When Saul was rejected by the Lord as king because of his disobedience, the Lord told Samuel to tell Saul:

> *"But now thy kingdom shall not continue: the LORD hath sought him a man after his own heart, and the LORD hath commanded him to be captain over his people, because thou hast not kept that which the LORD commanded thee."* 1 Samuel 13:14

Later, the Lord sent Samuel to the house of Jesse to anoint a new king. The youngest son, David, was not even invited in when his father brought the older brothers to meet the prophet Samuel. Nevertheless, this did not hinder the Lord or keep David from receiving that which the Lord had appointed for him to receive.

Fortunately, the prophet Samuel was one who knew the Lord and was led by His Spirit. As a child, Samuel had been brought to the temple and dedicated to the Lord. The first time the Lord spoke to him, it was a difficult word to share. Yet when Eli asked him what the Lord said, Samuel spoke all that the Lord told him (1 Samuel 3:18).

From that point in his childhood, he grew to become one of the greatest prophets in all of Israel. The Word tells us that none of Samuel's words fell to the ground (1 Samuel 3:19).

The Lord had told Samuel to stop mourning over Saul, who had been disobedient to the Lord, and to go to the house of Jesse, where he was to pour the horn of oil over that new thing God would yet do.

> *"And the LORD said unto Samuel, How long wilt thou mourn for Saul, seeing I have rejected him from reigning over Israel? fill thine horn with oil, and go, I will send thee to Jesse the Bethlehemite: for I have provided me a king among his sons."* 1 Samuel 16:1

Samuel, knowing the voice of the Lord and being sure he was in the right place, doing the right thing, at the right time, thought he knew who God was picking as he looked at Jesse's sons. Surely, he thought to himself, it is Eliab, standing here tall and handsome.

> *"But the LORD said unto Samuel, Look not on his countenance, or on the height of his stature; because I have refused him: for the LORD seeth not as man seeth; for man looketh on the outward appearance, but the LORD looketh on the heart."* 1 Samuel 16:7

Thankfully, Samuel did not stop at his own opinion, but heard the Lord say, "No, it is not Eliab; it is none of these." Knowing God had sent him to anoint someone, but realizing it was none of these, puzzled, he asked Jesse, "Do you have another son?"

Jesse sent for his youngest son, David, who was out in the fields caring for the sheep. Hurriedly, he was brought before Samuel. The Lord said, "This is the one!"

So Samuel took the horn of oil and poured it over David's head. (Regarding God's choice, notice in 1 Samuel 17:26-28 David's brother Eliab mocked, but David had faith when Goliath was challenging Israel!)

Later, an evil spirit was troubling Saul, so David was brought to the palace where he ministered to the Lord on his harp. As he did, Saul was comforted.

Yet jealousy rose up in Saul's heart against David, causing him to throw his javelin at David. That jealousy made him want to kill David, so David ended up hiding in order to stay alive.

Because of David's high regard for the anointing and the fact that Saul had been anointed as king, David refused to take action against Saul or retaliate in any way. He simply hid, as he waited in *trust* for the intervention of God.

> *"And he said unto his men, The LORD forbid that I should do this thing unto my master, the LORD's anointed, to stretch forth mine hand against him, seeing he is the anointed of the LORD."* 1 Samuel 24:6

This deep *trust* in God is seen also when his son Absalom was attempting to usurp his throne. His love for Absalom never wavered!

> *"And the king was much moved, and went up to the chamber over the gate, and wept: and as he went, thus he said, O my son Absalom, my son, my son Absalom! would God I had died for thee, O Absalom, my son, my son!"* 2 Samuel 18:33

When Shimei, one of Absalom's rebel friends was throwing stones at David, David refused to try to stop him. David so saw God over his life that he preferred to *trust* the Lord rather than defend himself.

> *"It may be that the LORD will look on mine affliction, and that the LORD will requite me good for his cursing this day."* 2 Samuel 16:12

David was far from perfect. Yet when he sinned, he repented and allowed the Lord to deal with him, again *trusting* himself into the hands of God.

> *"O LORD, take away the iniquity of thy servant; for I have done very foolishly ... I am in a great strait: let us fall now into the hand of the LORD; for his mercies are great: and let me not fall into the hand of man."* 2 Samuel 24:10b, 14

David is referred to twice in Scripture as a man after God's own heart. Later, when David's descendants prayed into promises God made to David, it is interesting to note they never mentioned his failures. They spoke of him only as God saw him, as they prayed into what God promised him, believing to be recipients of those blessings.

"Now therefore, O LORD God of Israel, keep with thy servant David my father that which thou hast promised him." 2 Chronicles 6:16a

We may never have a javelin thrown at us. Yet life gives each one opportunity to make choices.

When we are tested, the Lord will build in us a deep inner *trust* in Him if we are willing to look to Him in our circumstances, as David did, keeping our hearts right before Him. The Lord would even bring us into an identification with His heart in situations, for people, and also for the times we live in, as we are seeking His heart and desiring His heart to find expression in us.

During times of testing, may we continue to love others and above all, value the anointing in our own lives and in the lives of others. May that love and high regard for the anointing govern our words and the choices we make, as it keeps our hearts open to be recipients of all God's blessings that have been promised to those who have gone before us, as well as promises God would give us today.

Though circumstances may vary, this is the working that the Lord would do, not just in David, but in a people today, as the Lord prepares a people who He can use for His end-time glory. A people whose *trust* is in the Lord. A people who are keeping their hearts right before Him. A people who carry the very heart of God.

A people He can *trust* with authority, for they are under His authority. A people who are not moved by circumstances; circumstances are moved by them, because their *trust* is in the Lord. They simply walk day by day, endeavoring to keep their hearts right before Him. From that position, God is able to move in and through them.

David's one desire was to keep his heart right before the Lord and live in fellowship with Him. May this become the burning desire and prayer of our lives:

> *"One thing have I desired of the LORD, that will I seek after; that I may dwell in the house of the LORD all the days of my life, to behold the beauty of the LORD, and to enquire in his temple."* Psalm 27:4

A Passion to Please the Lord

"He shall see of the travail of his soul, and shall be satisfied." Isaiah 53:11

Some time ago, I was making a decision based on what I felt the Lord wanted. I saw how the Lord would bless others through my step of faith, but I was not receiving any understanding as to what was in store for me personally, and I became somewhat puzzled.

During a prior time of transition, I had received a specific word, then watched it unfold. This time, little was apparent regarding the impact on my own life. I wondered, was I missing something?

Then I understood! The Lord was simply doing something different this time. He was testing the motive of my heart. Was I obeying because something good was in store for me, like a puppy being led forward with a treat? Or was I obeying out of a pure desire to please the Lord, come what may?

This understanding brought tremendous peace, and though I had no "*promise*" concerning my own future, from the assurance that I had gained through years of walking with the Lord and knowing His faithfulness, I was able to rest in the fact that all would unfold at the right time, in the right way. And it did!

Paul said in Philippians 1:20, "*According to my earnest expectation and my hope, that in nothing I shall be ashamed, but that with all boldness, as always, so now also Christ shall be magnified in my body, whether it be by life, or by death.*"

I have often thought of the three Hebrew children. As they faced being thrown into a fiery furnace, they had no prophecy as to how all of that was going to turn out. It did not matter! There was a commitment in their life, and a faithfulness that governed their choices, come what may.

> "*If it be so, our God whom we serve is able to deliver us from the burning fiery furnace, and he will deliver us out of your hand, O king.*

> *But if not, be it known to you, O king, that we
> will not serve your gods, nor worship the
> golden image which you have set up."* Daniel
> 3:17-18

Years ago, an elderly lady with a profound walk with
the Lord brought me into contact with some writings
that spoke of a passionate love for Jesus, birthed from
a deeper revelation of the cross.

This awakened within me a longing to believe for what
I was hearing about: the birthing of a passion, like a
burning fire in the heart, that would create in all those
who were willing, an intense desire that the Man of
Calvary (*Jesus*) should be satisfied.

> *"He shall see of the travail of his soul, and
> shall be satisfied."* Isaiah 53:11

I knew it was from her own experience that she
spoke, as I heard that this passion would become so
strong, that it would become the dominating power
of a life, swallowing up all personal thought of
sacrifice or gain. How I longed and prayed for this

unveiling of the cross, that a deeper passion for the Lord might consume my own life.

John Wright Follette, the author of "Broken Bread," spoke of our love for Jesus becoming sufficient enough to allow the cancellation of our own lives for His life. As I heard him speak, a desire for my love for the Lord to grow to this dimension continued to well up within my own heart.

I began to understand the divine process which enables us to become that which the Lord desires. After the Holy Spirit comes upon us, as our life becomes submerged into His, we are enabled to "be," or "become" a witness unto the Lord.

> "But you shall receive power, after that the Holy Ghost is come upon you: and you shall be witnesses to me." Acts 1:8

This word "be" is a verb of being, not doing. The word "witness" also means "martyr." Brother Follette spoke of our life and personality coming under the dominion, power, and authority of the Holy Ghost, that we might *"be"* or *"become"* a witness (*martyr*) to Him. This is what we are to become, not do.

As I listened over and over to him speak of this divine process taking place, I prayed for this to take place in my own life, saying,

"Lord, cause my love for Jesus to become sufficient enough to allow the cancellation of my life, that I might become a living witness unto You. May my life become submerged into Yours. May Your Holy Spirit rule over me. *Cause* me Lord, by Your grace, to become the witness that You so desire (Ezekiel 36:27). I submit to Your working in my life. And please, do not pay any attention if I complain! This is what I want, and this is what I am praying for, with all my heart."

What a testimony Paul had:

> *"I am crucified with Christ: nevertheless I live; yet not I, but Christ lives in me: and the life which I now live in the flesh I live by the faith of the Son of God, who loved me, and gave Himself for me."* Galatians 2:20

Key elements to our being found faithful in the Lord's eyes are these two very things: a deeper revelation of the cross, with the birthing of a burning desire within to see the travail of His soul satisfied; and a love for Jesus that becomes strong enough to allow the cancellation of our own lives, that His life might be lived through our lives.

From these will come enduring commitment and true faithfulness, the place into which the Lord will bring those who are willing, today.

> *"For he is Lord of lords, and King of kings: and they that are with him are called, and chosen, and faithful."* Revelation 17:14

This requires a deep inner working of the Lord and perseverance on our part. Only God knows the heart. And the Lord will test us as to what truly motivates us. Is it self-motivation, or a desire to please Him?

The Lord is looking for those who will unconditionally surrender their lives to Him, come what may, whose singular passion is to please Him, to be found faithful in His sight, that His purpose might be fulfilled in and through their lives.

> *"Moreover it is required in stewards, that a man be found faithful."* 1 Corinthians 4:2

Our first call is to be with the Lord. As I spend quality time with the Lord and allow His working in my life, there will come a witness, or a change in my life. As my love increases for the Lord and the desire to see His soul satisfied grows, faithfulness will be birthed, not out of obligation, but from a burning passion for the Lord.

Divine substitution takes place. My love for the Lord begins to overcome all other desires and becomes the dominating factor in my life. The by-product is faithfulness, born from love.

> *"Be thou faithful unto death, and I will give thee a crown of life."* Revelation 2:10

My prayer for you is that the Lord will unveil Calvary to you in a deeper way, creating this singular, burning passion to please Him; that out of love, a deeper surrender to the Lord might be made.

This is the passion that will bring us through the days ahead, a commitment, from a singleness of heart, a sole desire to be found faithful, pleasing the Lord.

Even as Jesus was found faithful (Revelation 1:5), may passionate love birth commitment and faithfulness within each of us, that He might see of the travail of His soul and be satisfied.

A Call to Faithfulness

"Mine eyes shall be upon the faithful." Psalm 101:6

In the parable of the talents in Matthew 25:14-30, there are two types of servants. The one pleased the Lord and received a reward. The other did not! We want to be the type that pleases the Lord!

Regarding the servants that pleased the Lord, one servant had five talents; the other, two. Though the number of talents varied, the reward they received was identical. To both, the Lord said the same:

> *"Well done, good and faithful servant: you have been faithful over a few things, I will make you ruler over many things: enter you into the joy of your lord."* Matthew 25:21

Reward is not based on how much I have, but rather on being faithful with that which I have been entrusted. The Lord was displeased with the servant who had one talent, not because he only had one, but because he was not faithful in using wisely the one that he had been given (Matthew 25:27).

It does not matter if I have five talents, two, or one. What is important is that I am faithful in the place where I am, with that which the Lord has entrusted to me.

The word *"faithful"* is found at least eighty-two times in the Bible. The dictionary defines "faithful" as maintaining allegiance to someone or something; as being a constant, loyal friend.

Faithfulness also speaks of showing or having a strong sense of responsibility, of being conscientious, reliable, and full of faith.

> *"Moreover it is required in stewards, that a man be found faithful."* 1 Corinthians 4:2

The word *"required"* is a very strong word. To "require" means to demand, as being necessary or crucial. Of a steward, or servant, it is necessary, crucial, that he be found faithful.

Why is faithfulness so important? A key principle is found in Luke.

> "He that is faithful in that which is least is faithful also in much: and he that is unjust in the least is unjust also in much." Luke 16:10

The New Living Bible states it like this:

> "Unless you are faithful in small matters, you would not be faithful in large ones. If you cheat even a little, you would not be honest with greater responsibilities."

Revelation 2:10 speaks of those who are "faithful to death" as receiving a "crown of life."

Paul was able to say to Timothy, "I thank Christ Jesus our Lord, who has enabled me, for that he counted me faithful" (1 Timothy 1:12).

Paul goes on to speak of that which he was doing now, in contrast to that which he did prior to his conversion. What he was doing at the present time was marked by faithfulness. From that position, he was able to encourage Timothy also to be faithful.

My heart attitude is the key to my being faithful in whatever the Lord has called me to do. I am to do what I do out of a desire to please the Lord and be found faithful in His sight.

1 Corinthians 10:31 tells me, *"Whether therefore you eat, or drink, or whatsoever you do, do all to the glory of God."*

We all have different responsibilities. I may be called to cook, or to teach. Or I may be called to do construction work, or to work in an office. Perhaps I am a pastor, or a missionary, or maybe I have a ministry of helps. The reward is not for what I do. Rather, it is for my faithfulness in doing what I do. What matters is that I am faithful with that which the Lord has entrusted me.

I have held multiple positions at the same time, based on the setting I was in. I remember a time when in one setting, I was the pastor. In another, the song leader. In another, I set up and cleaned up. In another, I was simply a guest, with no other particular identity at all.

In each position I was just as happy, because I understood the reward was not for what I was doing, but for my *faithfulness* in whatever it was that I was doing, even if it meant just being a good guest. My contentment came from a deep inner desire simply to please the Lord and be found faithful in His eyes.

This simple understanding has changed my life. My purpose is no longer what I am "doing." My purpose is to *please the Lord*, in whatever it is I am called to do. I find myself doing things, but they stem from times spent with Him.

As the Lord continues to work in my life through circumstances and responsibilities that He has allowed, a working of the Holy Spirit continues, purifying my love for Him, increasing my desire to please Him. This love continues to grow, displacing all other desires. As a result, faithfulness is developed in my life.

At times I hear people say, if I could do this, or if I could do that, if I could be here, or go there, or have this, or have that, then I would be happy. That is not where true happiness lies. Happiness is in pleasing the Lord, where He has called you, doing what He has called you to do.

True happiness comes from that sense of being in right alignment with the Lord. True happiness comes simply from being faithful wherever, whatever.

Our lives all differ, yet we all have the same calling, to be with Him, that we might be or become a witness, first and foremost unto Him. When we understand that and are faithful to the calling, we are able to enter into the joy of the Lord.

God's Word says, "*Mine eyes shall be upon the faithful*" (Psalm 101:6).

Our part is simply to be faithful. He will do the rest.

Section 5
Our Calling

Strength and Encouragement

"My voice shalt thou hear in the morning, O LORD; in the morning will I direct my prayer unto thee, and will look up." Psalm 5:3

As I have been looking at the book of Revelation, I am reminded that the purpose of John's writing is to bring us into a deeper revelation of the Lord Jesus Christ and an understanding of the certain, beautiful, and victorious conclusion of God's plan of redemption.

In this world we have had tribulation, and turbulent times are increasing in this present dispensation. Yet scripture tells us of the posture we are to maintain in the midst of the days we are in.

"Lift up your heads; for your redemption draweth nigh." Luke 21:28b

If you walk through the book of Revelation, you will see "from start to finish," a people who are worshipping the Lord. We are called to be a part of this worship. True worship from the heart opens the door for the King of Glory to come in, in all His splendor.

"Lift up your heads, O ye gates; and be ye lift up, ye everlasting doors; and the King of glory shall come in." Psalm 24:7

Many have their eyes on the darkness about us. In an attitude of worship, we are to have our eyes on the Lord Jesus Christ, in earnest expectation of His glory shining forth in us and through us as never before in history.

"For, behold, the darkness shall cover the earth, and gross darkness the people: but the

LORD shall arise upon thee, and His glory shall be seen upon thee. And the Gentiles shall come to thy light, and kings to the brightness of thy rising." Isaiah 60:2-3

This is our calling today and in the coming days: simply to worship the Lord in expectation of His increasing presence in our midst. To "look up," that we might find His grace, strength, and wisdom; that His light might shine through us, that others too, might come to know the Lord's salvation.

The "parousia" of the Lord speaks of the "presencing" of the Lord which precedes the second coming of Christ. We are called to *be* a witness (Acts 1:8). The Lord is coming to be glorified and admired *in* His people (2 Thessalonians 1:10).

He is raising up today, a people "of His presence" as a witness or sample of the Lord Jesus Christ, that His presence might be made known, that others too, might come to see and know Christ.

Some may feel very alone in circumstances they are in. Yet the Lord has promised never to leave us or forsake us (Hebrews 13:5). He is a friend that sticks closer than a brother (Proverbs 18:24).

Yet, even beyond that, He is inviting us to become joined with Him in who He is and what He is doing today. There is no greater fellowship or fulfillment in this life. How often I think of Abraham, a man who knew God, who God moved through (Genesis 18). So the Lord desires for us to know Him and to become part of what He is doing today.

Though we may only see ourselves in the situations we are in today, and even feel alone at times, there is a multitude of overcomers the Lord is raising up, of which we are a part. There are places "marked by the presence of the Lord" that the Lord is establishing.

There is a choir of every nation, tongue, tribe, and people singing forth His praises today, both in heaven and on earth. As believers made one in Christ Jesus, we are very, very blessed to be part of such a people.

As Christians, we not only have much to be thankful for, there is an expectation and hope we carry in our hearts that goes beyond the circumstances of the day into that which is yet ahead.

My prayer is for the Lord to touch you afresh today, and each and every day, releasing fresh anointing, that you might walk with vision in the days ahead, strengthened and encouraged in the call of God that rests upon you.

Can we, together, make the following commitment?

"My voice shalt thou hear in the morning, O LORD; in the morning will I direct my prayer unto thee, and will look up." Psalm 5:3

Becoming a Witness

"And ye shall be witnesses unto me." Acts 1:8b

A quote from my dad, Wade Taylor, who is now with the Lord:

> "We are called to attain to the quality of the life of Jesus. In 'that day' when we stand before Him at the Judgment Seat of Christ, our life will be 'measured' against His life. We will not be graded 'quantitatively' by all that we have accomplished, but rather 'qualitatively' by what we have become."

Embracing this simple yet profound truth has changed my life. It's wonderful the things I have been able to "do" through the years, as at times I have served as an administrator, teacher, missionary, or pastor, and presently, as I oversee www.wadetaylor.org and Parousia Ministries.

Yet, more important, is what I have "become" while doing these things. Even more important: What am I "becoming" *today* through choices I am making now? Am I maturing spiritually? Am I allowing my self-life to be dealt with, that increasingly more of Christ might be seen in me? Am I just talking about the Lord, or is His life being formed in me and seen through my actions and words?

We are to *be* a witness unto Him! (Acts 1:8 KJV) As He is, so are we to *be* in the world! (1 John 4:17) This focus, not on accomplishments, but on *becoming* "as He is" has absolutely changed my life and continues to challenge me day by day. How often we miss this life-changing truth and the present working of the Holy Spirit. Without this, what I "do" may benefit others, but it will not necessarily benefit me.

> *"I am become as sounding brass, or a tinkling cymbal ... I am nothing ... it profiteth me nothing."* 1 Corinthians 13:1-3

My prayer today is this: That as He is, so we will be. That we will so yield our lives to the Lord Jesus Christ and so allow His Holy Spirit to work within our hearts, that we will not be the same people we were yesterday, but each day, we will be more like Christ.

> *"Herein is our love made perfect, that we may have boldness in the day of judgment: because as he is, so are we in this world."* 1 John 4:17

Not everything that happens in this life is good. However, Romans 8:26-27 speaks of the intercession of the Holy Spirit for us; then in verse 28, God promises He will take "all things" and work them together for our good as we set our love on Him. Verse 29 goes on to say, *"For whom he foreknew, he also predestined to be conformed to the image of his Son, that he might be the firstborn among many brothers"* (WEB).

When I truly saw Christ's intercession for me and this great potential, what before were just mundane or, at times, even painful situations, became opportunities, as I learned to yield my heart to the Lord in trust, allowing His Spirit to work inside of me.

Song of Solomon 8:5 asks, *"Who is this that cometh up from the wilderness, leaning on her beloved?"*

"The wilderness" speaks of a place of testing. "Leaning" speaks of a reliance on the Lord Jesus Christ. As we learn to submit our lives to Him, it becomes no longer our old nature, desires, reactions, or opinions that rule us, but His nature, as "who He is" finds expression through us.

What a testimony as we grow into becoming like Him. We become one with Him!

> *"Neither pray I for these alone, but for them also which shall believe on me through their word; that they all may be one; as thou, Father, art in me, and I in thee, that they also may be one in us: that the world may believe that thou hast sent me."* John 17:20-21

As I learn to value and invite the Lord's work in my life and you allow the Lord to work in you, that which brings disunity is washed away, and in Christ Jesus, we are made one.

"But if we walk in the light, as he is in the light, we have fellowship one with another, and the blood of Jesus Christ his Son cleanseth us from all sin." 1 John 1:7

As a redeemed people made one in Christ Jesus, may we find ourselves a part of those singing this new song:

"Thou art worthy to take the book, and to open the seals thereof: for thou wast slain, and hast redeemed us to God by thy blood out of every kindred, and tongue, and people, and nation; And hast made us unto our God kings and priests: and we shall reign on the earth." Revelation 5:9-10

The Lord's desire is that together we will *become* a witness and testimony of the Lord Jesus Christ in every circumstance or place we find ourselves (Acts 1:8).

Jesus is coming back to be seen and admired *in* a people! (2 Thessalonians 1:10).

"And every man that has this hope inside him purifies himself, even as he is pure." 1 John 3:3

How do we purify ourselves? Through the choices we make. How do we make right choices? Jesus promised He would not leave us without strength (John 14:18). The Holy Spirit, who lives inside those who believe, gives discernment and reveals truth. He gives us strength to make right choices. We make these choices until, before long, it becomes not just my "choice" but my very "nature" to respond even as Jesus would respond. "As He is" so we are experientially becoming.

Salvation is a gift (Ephesians 2:8). Character is formed. We are called to be partakers of His divine nature (2 Peter 1:4). This is the work of the Holy Spirit today — the formation of Christ *in* us, the hope of glory (Colossians 1:27)!

Judicially, I am saved through faith. Experientially, I am "becoming" as He is! From that position, I will "do" certain things, but they will flow from what I have "become."

My witness is what I am becoming. Paul said, *"Not as though I had already attained, either were already perfect: but I follow after, if that I may apprehend that for which also I am apprehended of Christ Jesus"* (Philippians 3:12).

Today, may we yield to the ministry of the Holy Spirit, that we might, moment by moment, make right choices, as we allow the Lord to work within our hearts. He must increase! We must decrease (John 3:30), so more of Jesus is seen in us.

Identification with Him

"Herein is our love made perfect, that we may have boldness in the day of judgment: because as he is, so are we in this world." 1 John 4:17

What a powerful statement! John is stating that because of the working of the Lord within (love being made perfect in our lives), who we are and what we do is now a reflection of the very life of the Lord Jesus Christ. As He is, so are we! Because of that, we will be able to stand before His throne one day, not in fear, but in confidence.

Our calling as Christians is simply to "be" as He is. We were never called to "do" witnessing. We were called to "be" a witness to the "uttermost part of the earth," or in every situation and place we might find ourselves (Acts 1:8).

We can "be" or "become" a witness unto the Lord as we yield to His inward working, which often takes place through our daily circumstances. The very life of

Christ is worked into our innermost being as we seek to respond in ways that please the Lord. Through this process, we "become" as He is. From that place of identity with Him, He can then express Himself through us, doing that which He desires, not only *in* us, but through our lives.

There is a place of *identification* that the Lord is calling us up into, where His heart has been so formed in us that it is no longer "I" but Christ who is seen in me (Galatians 2:20). The *very nature of Christ* becomes my nature through identification with Him. I learn to respond as He would respond, rather than just in my own way. As I do this, I am brought into an *identity* with Him. I begin to experience the very life of Christ. As a result, others can see His life through me.

This is portrayed in the life of Abraham, who, going through many tests and trials, came into a place of knowing the very heart of God. In that knowing, Abraham was able to express God's heart when he heard that judgment was about to fall on Sodom and Gomorrah.

Abraham was sitting in the door of his tent (Genesis 18:1) when the Lord came. Though there were unfilled promises in Abraham's life that he could have begun to question the Lord about, that was not his response. Instead, he proceeded to minister to the Lord (v. 5).

As Abraham ministered to the Lord, at His own initiative, the Lord did speak into Abraham's life regarding the promise yet to be fulfilled (v. 10). But the Lord did not stop there; He then said, "*Shall I hide from Abraham that thing which I do?*" (v. 17).

Then the Lord shared with Abraham His intention to visit Sodom and Gomorrah. He told Abraham that a great cry was coming to Him from Sodom and Gomorrah because of the grievousness of their sin (v. 20). The Lord said He was going to go visit Sodom and Gomorrah and see if, in fact, they were doing according to the cry He was hearing; if they were not, He would know it (v. 21).

Abraham knew there was great sin in that city, so he knew what the Lord was going to find when He visited there. Knowing the righteousness of God, he knew that meant judgment. But Abraham also knew the heart of God.

Understanding that a visitation was coming which would result in judgment, but also knowing the heart of God, Abraham began to make intercession. He prayed that the righteous would not die with the wicked when judgment came. Scripture tells us it was because of Abraham's prayers that Lot was brought out before judgment fell (Genesis 19:29).

Abraham is referred to as a friend of God in scripture (James 2:23). Looking at his life, he was one who recognized the Lord's presence and responded quickly with acts of worship. He had a listening ear to which God could speak. Because he not only knew God's heart, but was willing to *identify* with God's heart in intercession, God was able to use Abraham in sparing Lot.

When Abraham understood what was about to happen, he did not respond just according to his own thoughts or opinions. He positioned himself according to the heart of God. He *identified* with God's heart, then interceded accordingly. What joy he must have experienced when Lot was spared!

Today the Lord is calling us into the experience of *godly caring and concern*, where His love can be visibly seen through our lives, be it through prayer, caring words, or kind deeds. As we give of ourselves for others, the shared *joy* we experience when we have participated in meeting their need is worth far more than all we may ever give in their behalf.

> *"For what is our hope, or joy, or crown of rejoicing? Are not even ye in the presence of our Lord Jesus Christ at his coming? For ye are our glory and joy."* 1 Thessalonians 2:19-20

When I was pastoring in the Washington, D.C., area, we experienced a major blizzard. Each time we shoveled, more snow came. Men from the church were trying to help, but they were needed to deal with the snow at their own homes, plus the roads were slippery and difficult to drive on, and it was almost impossible for them to get to the church.

My dad was there for a conference we had scheduled for that weekend. We called everyone we knew, telling them not to come. However, we still wanted to go ourselves, just in case someone did come; but in order to get there, we had to shovel our driveway.

A snowplow had cleared the main road, leaving a *huge* bank of snow at the foot of our drive. My dad came out to help shovel, but when I questioned him, he admitted the strain was causing him some discomfort. "Don't worry," I told him, "I love to shovel snow. You go inside, and I will take care of this." And there I was, left alone with my shovel. Now, I think he went in and began to pray.

As I shoveled, I remembered that it had cost about $300 to have the driveway and parking lot plowed, only to again be buried in snow. I could not afford that, so I kept shoveling. It was a wet, heavy snow, and my efforts were barely making a dent. As I shoveled and prayed, I found myself quickened with a passage of scripture from the Song of Solomon.

"Come, my beloved, let us go forth into the field ... there will I give thee my loves." Song of Solomon 7:11-12

I knew that the Lord had called me to the place where I was and that we were in His vineyard together. "There will I give thee my loves" echoed in my heart as I continued shoveling. "Lord," I said, "It is not that I am not willing to shovel this snow, but it is too much for me; it's too heavy. Couldn't You show me Your loves? Couldn't You send a plow to clear this snow?"

At that moment, I looked up, and there was a white truck with a yellow plow passing by on the other side of the road, right in front of me. I felt the quickening of the Holy Spirit, which caused me to jump, my arms going up like I was in a worship service, as I said "Oh!"

The driver of the truck saw me and thought I was waving at him. He turned around, came back, and without a word, began to clear our driveway. As I watched his expertise in plowing, my heart sank. I remembered the $300 and thought, "Now what have I done?"

Then I noticed a Christian bumper sticker on the back of his truck. When he finished, he would not accept any money. As I insisted, he said next time we could give him $25 if we wanted to. For the rest of the time we lived there, we never again had to shovel snow. I still marvel and thank the Lord every time I think of that.

When I shared this experience with our church, everyone was happy. *But it was the ones who had come and fellowshipped with me in my shoveling who were the happiest.* They knew what that snowplow meant, because they had tried to help shovel!

As we give our lives to pray for and to help others, there is a *joy* we share with the Lord in what He does. Some years ago we heard that a minister we knew had come into a higher realm of ministry.

Everyone rejoiced at the news, but I was really excited because I had prayed and interceded for them. Later they said to me, "I believe it was your prayers that caused this to happen." I don't know about that, but I do know I had a part, and that gave me great *joy*.

We are to edify others and minister grace to them. There are times in a person's life when their need is exposed and seen by others. There are also many different extremes in today's lifestyles. The Lord does not call us to condemn or judge; rather, He calls us to love.

The love with which God loves us is the same love He is calling us to love others with. This is the love which the Lord desires to form in our spirit, that we might be *partakers of His divine nature,* learning to share with Him in His love for others, that we might also share in His *joy*.

> *"And we have known and believed the love that God hath to us. God is love; and he that dwelleth in love dwelleth in God, and God in him."* 1 John 4:16

May this dimension of who God is utterly transform us, changing our thinking, bringing us into an *identification* with the Lord. Let us be willing to give up our lives, whether by spending time in prayer, speaking kind words, or doing kind deeds. May the ministry of the Holy Spirit come forth from *within* us, so that God's love will be shed abroad through us.

May we be like Abraham, ones who know the Lord and who are quick to respond to His presence. May we be ones who know the heart of God, ones to whom the Lord can speak.

May we be ones who will *identify* with the Lord and His heart in intercession.

Even as Lot was brought out before judgment fell, there is an end-time harvest yet to come. What *joy* we will have when we realize we have had a part, as we have been willing to find the heart of God for this hour, then *identify* with His heart in intercession.

Living Epistles

"Now thanks be to God who always leads us in triumph in Christ, and through us diffuses the fragrance of His knowledge in every place."

2 Corinthians 2:14 NKJV

We were extremely blessed and encouraged by the testimony of a young man with a beautiful family, who we recently visited. He said the Lord touched his life through teachings he heard when he was in eighth grade. What he heard changed his life and gave him a hunger for more. Today his life is different because of the relationship he has come into with the Lord.

Others have noticed this difference and ask him why he is different. He is able to tell them it is because his life is in God's hands; his faith and trust is in the Lord. They wonder why he has peace even during uncertain times. He tells them he knows God loves him and has a plan for his life. He trusts the Lord and His faithfulness. Then he shares that they too can know the Lord, and put their trust in Him.

We are living in uncertain and stressful times. How can we help? One way is by living upright lives regardless of what challenges we may face, that there might be godly examples for others to see and find encouragement in.

Paul speaks of our *lives* as being an *"epistle ... known and read of all men"* (2 Corinthians 3:2). Our *being* this *"witness"* is an important aspect of the high calling of God resting upon our lives. We must consider how our "sermon" is being preached.

As I consecrate my life to the Lord, making Him my first priority, the fragrance of His presence will mark my life. God's desire is that we abide in Christ, so His life can be seen through us.

Allowing who Christ is, to find expression in our life experiences, will absolutely transform us. It will also touch others.

Regardless of occupation or location, there are those who are reading our lives. As we live credible lives people will be more willing to listen to our words. As we become carriers of His presence, His presence within us will flow out and touch others, beyond what words alone ever could.

Jesus came as the very expression of God's love. His mission was not to be served, but to serve and give His life for others (Matthew 20:28). He sought no reward or recognition from man. His sole desire was simply to please His heavenly Father.

Because of that, it did not matter to Him if He was speaking to one Samaritan woman at a well (John 4:7) or to five thousand people, as when He multiplied the loaves and the fishes (Matthew 14:21). Jesus was able to be led and to be used wherever He was needed.

As we live in communion with the Lord and out of a desire to please Him, a purity of motive is formed within us. We do what we do, simply out of a conviction that it is what the Lord would have us do, and a desire to please Him.

When we are doing what God has called us to do, then no one thing is more glorious than another. It does not matter if we are seen or appreciated. The Lord sees and cares, and His satisfaction is all that matters. We live to please Him.

The Lord is raising up a people, *Living Epistles*, who will touch every sphere of life. May we be found faithful to His leading, wherever that might take us, and whatever we might find ourselves doing. May our single desire be to please the Lord.

Paul speaks of our lives as being *"living epistles,"* not written with ink but with the Spirit of the living God.

> *"Forasmuch as ye are manifestly declared to be the epistle of Christ ministered by us, written not with ink, but with the Spirit of the living God; not in tables of stone, but in fleshy tables of the heart."* 2 Corinthians 3:3

As we submit our lives to the Lord Jesus Christ and allow His inner working, we become a sample of Christ. Regardless of what our hands might be doing, may the peace and love of Christ within us be sensed by and minister to others, as Jesus is seen in and through our lives.

> *"Herein is our love made perfect, that we may have boldness in the day of judgment: because as he is, so are we in this world."* 1 John 4:17

True joy is simply in pleasing God's heart as we do His will and are found faithful.

> *"His lord said unto him, Well done, good and faithful servant ... enter thou into the joy of thy lord."* Matthew 25:21, 23

May the pages of our lives be pleasing unto the Lord, as they are seen and read by others. May the love of Jesus and the fragrance of His presence be made known through our lives. May we be found faithful!

This is the high calling of God that rests on each of our lives.

A Present Purpose

"Blessed are they that keep his testimonies, and that seek him with the whole heart." Psalm 119:2

There are many mixed voices today, sending different messages and giving different advice. This we can be sure of: Today is the day of preparation. Today is the day I have, to make right choices. Today is the day the Holy Spirit desires to do a deeper work in me, that Christ might be seen and glorified in my life.

"Christ in you, the hope of glory." Colossians 1:27

Scripture makes it very clear that Jesus is coming back to be seen and admired *"in"* a people.

"When he shall come to be glorified in his saints, and to be admired in all them that believe..." 2 Thessalonians 1:10

As we allow the Lord to deal with our self-life, more and more of Jesus is seen in us. This is our testimony and our witness.

> *"I am crucified with Christ: nevertheless I live; yet not I, but Christ liveth in me."* Galatians 2:20

Acts 1:8 tells us we are to *"be"* a witness. After the Holy Spirit comes upon me, through His power I am enabled to "be" or "become" a witness, or a sample of the Lord Jesus Christ.

> *"But ye shall receive power, after that the Holy Ghost is come upon you: and ye shall be witnesses unto me ... unto the uttermost part of the earth."* Acts 1:8

The verb in this verse is a present imperative, or an action verb, which speaks of a process of transformation after I have been born again then filled with the Holy Spirit. This empowering enables me to "be" or "become" a witness, wherever I might be, to the uttermost parts of the earth.

There is always a progression in that which the Lord does. In the Old Testament, the Holy Spirit would come upon an individual to "do" a particular thing or to fulfill a special calling.

Yet in the New Testament, we see the Holy Spirit coming to empower a corporate body of believers to "be" or "become" a witness unto the Lord. From this state of being, we then do what we do, which is our service; but the empowering in the New Covenant goes beyond "doing," to "becoming" a witness unto the Lord.

In the Old Testament, the children of Israel were called to be a witness, but they lacked the grace or the empowerment to fulfill their calling. In the New Testament, we have that grace through the empowerment of the Holy Spirit.

> "A new heart also will I give you ... and I will put my spirit within you, and cause you to walk in my statutes." Ezekiel 36:26-27

What a privilege to live in the day we are in! To be a New Covenant body of believers! What grace (empowerment) is available to us today, if we will but reach out for it!

Today, where there is uncertainty, conflict, and fear, there is an assurance we can demonstrate in Christ Jesus. Some see only man's systems failing; yet others understand God's purposes are moving forward. In the midst of all that is happening, there is a people being empowered by the Holy Spirit to be a witness unto the Lord today.

Following the crucifixion of Jesus, the early church was in confusion and fear. After the resurrected Christ appeared to the disciples, their whole perspective changed. Even in the midst of great pressure, they were able to see the sovereignty of God and focus on His purpose being fulfilled, as they asked for boldness to declare the Word of God.

"The kings of the earth stood up, and the rulers were gathered together against the Lord, and against his Christ ... for to do whatsoever thy hand and thy counsel determined before to be done. And now,

Lord, behold their threatenings: and grant unto thy servants, that with all boldness they may speak thy word." Acts 4:26-29

In the presence of the risen Lord, the fact of His sovereignty became a reality to the early church. From that point on, circumstances no longer caused them to become fearful or confused. They stood boldly in their witness of the resurrected Jesus, even to the point of death.

"Parousia" is a New Testament Greek word that relates to the second coming of Christ; this word also relates to the "Presencing" of the Lord, in which He is beginning to reveal Himself in a greater and more personal way to those who have come apart to seek Him.

The Lord is manifesting His presence and making Himself known today to those who are seeking Him, that we might be empowered in our day, just as the early disciples were empowered in the time in which they lived.

In order to receive this empowering, our times of worship, prayer, and spending time in God's Word in communion and fellowship with Him, are essential.

Jesus is our example. Revelation 3:21 makes us aware that we can overcome even as He overcame:

> *"To him that overcometh will I grant to sit with me in my throne, even as I also overcame, and am set down with my Father in his throne."*

If Jesus had used His deity to overcome, we could not overcome as He overcame, because we are not deity and never will be.

How did Jesus overcome? He did not use His deity. Neither did He rely on mere human strength. There was a divine enabling that Jesus received, which strengthened Him to overcome.

We see this clearly in the garden of Gethsemane prior to His crucifixion. Jesus went into the garden and prayed, then He prayed, then He prayed again; and an angel came and strengthened Him.

"And there appeared an angel unto him from heaven, strengthening him." Luke 22:43

That same divine enabling is available to us today, if we will but reach out for it.

"But they that wait upon the LORD shall renew their strength; they shall mount up with wings as eagles; they shall run, and not be weary; and they shall walk, and not faint." Isaiah 40:31

The word "renew" in this verse translates "exchange." There is an exchange of strength available, a divine enabling, for those who are willing to take the time to receive it.

All through Scripture we are taught not only to pray, but to continue in prayer and to pray through. As we spend time in prayer, opening our hearts to the Lord, we receive deeper revelation of the Lord Jesus Christ and the strength to stand by His Spirit.

In the time of transition from law into grace, prior to His crucifixion, Jesus said:

"This is your hour, and the power of darkness." Luke 22:53

In the midst of that darkness, Jesus was able to say that though the prince of this world came, he was unable to find anything in Him, except that He loved and obeyed His heavenly Father.

"For the prince of this world cometh, and hath nothing in me. But that the world may know that I love the Father; and as the Father gave me commandment, even so I do." John 14:30-31

Likewise, today we are seeing the power of darkness, this time in its final hour. Yet the Lord is preparing a people in whom Jesus is being seen and admired; a people in whom the prince of this world, who works through children of disobedience (Ephesians 2:2), can find nothing but love and obedience to the Lord.

"And they overcame him by the blood of the Lamb, and by the word of their testimony; and they loved not their lives unto the death." Revelation 12:11

The Lord will not leave Himself without a witness. Jesus came as the perfect Witness. Now, as New Covenant believers, we have divine enablement available to us to be that witness through the power of His Holy Spirit.

I often talk about the preparation of a people for the end-time purposes of the Lord. For those who are willing, this is the preparation that the Lord would do *today* for His end-time purpose: He would prepare a people in whom Jesus can be seen and admired, everywhere and in every circumstance; a people in whom no test, no pressure, no problem can cause anything to be seen but love and obedience to the Lord Jesus Christ.

What a calling!

Section 6
Living in His Presence

His Dwelling Place

"That I may win Christ, and be found in him..." Philippians 3:8-9

I once heard someone say, "You are as close to God as you want to be!" I was shocked. I had always yearned for an ever-closer relationship with the Lord. At times, I looked at others who had a strong sense of God's presence in their lives and thought how fortunate they were that God had chosen them for such a beautiful relationship with Himself.

Yet, as I thought about it, I had to acknowledge that what I had heard was true, I was as close to God as *I chose* to be. It was me, not Him, making that choice.

In Genesis, when God created man, it was for a time of fellowship with Him. Adam and Eve were given responsibilities, then, in the cool of the evening, the Lord would come to fellowship with them.

> *"And the LORD God took the man, and put him into the garden of Eden to dress it and to keep it."* Genesis 2:15

> *"And they heard the voice of the LORD God walking in the garden in the cool of the day..."* Genesis 3:8a

Yet, the day came when they disobeyed God. Then, because of sin, instead of being able to respond to the Lord and His coming as they had in times past, they now hid from the presence of the Lord.

> *"Adam and his wife hid themselves from the presence of the LORD God amongst the trees of the garden."* Genesis 3:8b

God did not leave man in that state of separation from Himself, but made a way for reconciliation, that fellowship might be restored between God and man.

> *"And the LORD God called unto Adam, and said unto him, Where art thou?"* Genesis 3:9

> *"Unto Adam also and to his wife did the LORD God make coats of skins, and clothed them."* Genesis 3:21

The Lord God Almighty is omniscient; He knows all things. He knew Adam and Eve had disobeyed. He knew they were hiding. Yet God called out to man in redemptive love, enabling man to respond in a confession, which is the beginning of repentance and the restoration of fellowship with God.

God clothed Adam and Eve in coats of skin, the first shedding of blood we have record of in scripture. Today, because of the precious blood of Jesus shed for us, we too, clothed in His love and grace, can live and walk in His presence, as well as enjoy quality times alone with the Lord in communion and intimate fellowship with Him.

"Let us therefore come boldly unto the throne of grace, that we may obtain mercy, and find grace to help in time of need." Hebrews 4:16

In repentance, I take my first step toward fellowship with the Lord Jesus Christ through faith in His atoning sacrifice, and His love for me. I come to know the power of His blood, which cleanses me and gives me new life. In faith, I can now come boldly before the throne of God, accepting what Christ has done for me on Calvary.

Scripture tells me I have been saved, not through good things I have done, but by grace, through the washing of regeneration and renewing of the Holy Spirit:

"For by grace are ye saved through faith; and that not of yourselves: it is the gift of God: Not of works, lest any man should boast." Ephesians 2:8-9

"Not by works of righteousness which we have done, but according to his mercy he saved us, by the washing of regeneration, and renewing of the Holy Ghost." Titus 3:5

Jesus said in John 3:7, "*Marvel not that I said unto thee, Ye must be born again.*"

The above verses speak of this new birth, or of being born again. The *washing of regeneration* is the cleansing work of the Spirit of God within a life, making a person new in a moment of time, as the Holy Spirit imparts spiritual life into the one who believes.

Through this regeneration of the Holy Spirit, scripture says I now am a *new creature* in Christ Jesus.

> "*Therefore if any man be in Christ, he is a new creature: old things are passed away; behold, all things are become new.*" 2 Corinthians 5:17

As a "*newborn babe*" (1 Peter 2:2), I am able to enter into a new fellowship with God, through the Holy Spirit that now dwells inside me.

> "*Jesus answered and said unto him, Verily, verily, I say unto thee, Except a man be born again, he cannot see the kingdom of God.*" John 3:3

Within mankind there is an emptiness that can be filled only with God Himself. This emptiness causes a desire or a hunger inside, that man seeks to fill in many ways. But only God can fill that space, because it was created for God Himself to dwell in.

I have been created with an instinctive hunger for God, but when I am saved, or born again, that hunger increases. Even as a newborn babe cries out to be fed, as a new creation, my spiritual capacity is enlarged and my spirit man longs for nourishment.

That hunger is a key to my spiritual growth and to coming into a deeper fellowship with the Lord as He draws me to Himself. The Lord will do His part: He will draw us.

> *"Draw me, we will run after thee."* Song of Solomon 1:4a

Within each of us has been created the ability to respond. But now I must make the choice either to cultivate the hunger the Lord has formed within me and allow it to grow, becoming filled with the Lord

Himself through times of fellowship with Him ... or ignore it.

If I am going to come into a deeper fellowship with the Lord, there are choices I must make. Am I going to respond to the Lord's drawing? Am I going to make time to feed that hunger? Or am I going to allow other things to stifle it?

These are choices I must make if I am going to grow in the things of the Lord. I must make time to feed on God's word, spend time in prayer, and fellowship with other Christians:

> "As newborn babes, desire the sincere milk of the word, that ye may grow thereby." 1 Peter 2:2

> "Lord, teach us to pray." Luke 11:1

> "Not forsaking the assembling of ourselves together..." Hebrews 10:25

Yet, it is not mere "religious activity" that will deepen my fellowship with the Lord. It is not merely going to church once a week, or even twice. It is not just the maintenance of a devotional time, where I have formed the daily discipline of reading my Bible and praying a prayer. The Lord's desire goes beyond just a religious routine.

While all of these things are a part of God's plan for spiritual growth, there is still something *more* the Lord is looking for, that brings deeper meaning even into these disciplines. The longing of the Lord is for me to grow in my *fellowship* with Him.

As I am spending time with the Lord, not as religious habit, but in *communion* with a personal God who knows me and loves me and desires to be known, I will grow closer to God in my own personal *fellowship* and *relationship* with Him.

He has called me and already shown me the way through His word and the guidance of His Holy Spirit. But I have to make the choice! How close do I want to be? How much time am I willing to invest? How focused do I want to become? Am I willing to pay the price to *"win Christ, and be found in Him"* (Philippians 3:8, 9)?

Salvation is a free gift. But that which follows is not free; there is a price to be paid if we are going to enter into the fullness of His desire for our lives. It requires choice! And the choices are not always easy to make.

> *"Yea doubtless, and I count all things but loss for the excellency of the knowledge of Christ Jesus my Lord: for whom I have suffered the loss of all things, and do count them but dung, that I may win Christ. And be found in him."*
> Philippians 3:8-9a

There are two aspects to the time that I spend with the Lord. One is quality times apart, alone in His presence. The other is my daily walk, as I learn to maintain fellowship with Him throughout my day. I learn to share all of life's experiences with Him.

Some have called this "practicing His presence." Scripture refers to it as *"abiding in Him"* (John 15:4-7). In essence, I train myself to be more mindful of the Lord and His presence, not religiously, but in an ongoing fellowship with Him, out of a hunger to know Him and serve Him more fully.

"Casting down imaginations, and every high thing that exalteth itself against the knowledge of God, and bringing into captivity every thought to the obedience of Christ." 2 Corinthians 10:5

"That I may know him, and the power of his resurrection, and the fellowship of his sufferings, being made conformable unto his death." Philippians 3:10

In 1 Thessalonians 5:17, scripture speaks of praying *"without ceasing."* How can I pray without ceasing? I do this as I learn to maintain *communion* with God, regardless of the activity I am engaged in. Everything we do can be time spent with the Lord, as we maintain an *attitude of worship*, inviting Him to be a part, staying mindful of Him in all we do.

If my attitude is right and I maintain the poise of my spirit, I can pray while I am driving the car, cutting the grass, or washing the dishes.

However, I cannot pray when I am worrying, holding resentment, or preoccupied with thoughts not about

God. The same part of me that prays can become busy with these other things, interfering with the fellowship I am being called to continually maintain.

The Lord is calling us up into a clearing of our lives: faith rather than worry, forgiveness rather than resentment. To maintain a poise of spirit that is toward Him.

As we come into this, we will be able to pray without ceasing, practice His presence, abide in Him — whatever you might want to call it, *our lives will be marked by the fragrance of His presence*.

"Abide in me, and I in you." John 15:4a

"Now he uses us to spread the knowledge of Christ everywhere, like a sweet perfume." 2 Corinthians 2:14c NLT

It is my choice to set aside these other things so He might have more freedom to manifest Himself in and through my life. That we might become a people, in whom the Lord can be who *He* wants to be, and do what *He* wants to do!

"Christ in you, the hope of glory!" Colossians 1:27b

This is the Kingdom of God established, God sitting on His throne in the hearts of His people, as His glory shines forth into the darkness round about, bringing light and hope.

There is a "habitation of God" being established in the earth, where His government can flow out, that His glory might be made known. This happens through a people who have made themselves available to Him. These have become activated, not through man's methods, but God's, as His power is released from within.

> *"In whom all the building fitly framed together groweth unto an holy temple in the Lord: In whom ye also are builded together for an habitation of God through the Spirit."* Ephesians 2:21-22

That corporate habitation of God being built together begins with you and me, and the choices we make. The Lord will manifest His presence in lives fully submitted to Him. Christ, glorified *in* His saints! Admired *in* all them that believe! Christ desires to be seen and glorified *in* you and *in* me! (Colossians 1:27b; 2 Thessalonians 1:10)

As a people who hunger for more than they are experiencing or seeing today, begin to set themselves apart, the Lord will begin to move more manifestly. He waits for us, that He might move in a greater way.

> *"Turn ye unto me, saith the LORD of hosts, and I will turn unto you, saith the LORD of hosts."* Zechariah 1:3b

A familiar song says longingly, "Just a closer walk with Thee, grant it Jesus is my plea..."

It is available, if we will but make the choice!

Desiring His Presence Above All Else

"My soul longeth, yea, even fainteth for the courts of the LORD: my heart and my flesh crieth out for the living God." Psalm 84:2

Years ago, I asked the Lord that if I ever were to have a ministry, it would be marked by His presence. This continues to be my desire today. First and foremost, I want the presence of the Lord to mark my own life, but also any corporate gatherings that I might be responsible for.

I've mentioned a little song that I have loved for many years: "For I was born to be Thy dwelling place, a home for the presence of the Lord. So let my life now be separated Lord to Thee, that I might be what I was born to be." This continues to be my desire.

We must be well established in the "fact" of God's presence. Psalms 139:7–12 makes it clear, the Lord is omnipresent. As Jonah found out, there is nowhere we can go to flee from His presence.

Yet scripture also speaks of the "manifest" presence of God. The word manifest speaks of the Lord revealing, or making Himself known in such a way that His presence is apparent even to our natural senses.

> *"He that hath my commandments, and keepeth them, he it is that loveth me: and he that loveth me shall be loved of my Father, and I will love him, and will manifest myself to him" John 14:21*

I began this book by talking about a "revelation of a relationship." I've mentioned Hattie Hammond numbers of times because the Lord used her to "open my eyes" to see a love relationship, which we too can have with the Lord. There came a hunger inside me, for more than I was experiencing at the time.

I also saw the beauty of a life deeply embedded with worship. There was an atmosphere of worship that I sensed when I was near her, something which went beyond words. I remember one occasion, when I was blessed to drive her home. She was sitting silently next to me, yet an atmosphere of worship filled the car; the sense of God's presence was tangible. Later, I realized that worshipful atmosphere was her home; the place where she was accustomed to living.

Isaiah 6 speaks of the Lord sitting upon a throne and his train filling the temple. In that presence of God, as worship declared His holiness, the posts of the door moved, and the house was filled with smoke. That smoke speaks of the glory of the Lord. In that glory Isaiah, a prophet, experienced a further repentance, then he was given a word to speak.

As we value the presence of the Lord, and take time to spend time with Him, He will reveal, or make Himself known to us. In His presence, as we behold him, we are changed by His spirit. 2 Corinthians speaks of being changed from glory to glory. This inner change brings us into a deeper place of fellowship with the Lord.

> "But we all, with open face beholding as in a glass the glory of the Lord, are changed into the same image from glory to glory, even as by the Spirit of the Lord." 2 Corinthians 3:18

As the Lord is invited into our lives and His throne is established within our hearts, the peace of His presence will not only fill our lives, but begin to impact those about us. This becomes my daily experience as I learn to maintain my fellowship with Him throughout the day, sharing all of life's experiences with Him. I learn to abide in Him, as He abides in me.

We are to seek the Lord with all our hearts. His presence is not just "an experience." His presence is what surrounds Him, where He is welcome and His throne has been established.

As this desire for the presence of the Lord has grown in my life, I have been encouraged by the life of Moses.

As the Lord was establishing the tabernacle of Moses, He said,

> *"And I will dwell among the children of Israel, and will be their God."* Exodus 29:45

Later, the children of Israel grieved the Lord. Because of this, though the Lord was still going to use Moses and allow him to lead Israel to Canaan, He said to Moses,

> *"Depart and go ... and I will send My Angel before you ... to a land flowing with milk and honey; for I will not go up in your midst ... for you are a stiff-necked people."* Exodus 33:1-3 NKJV

But Moses desired something much more than merely coming into "a land that flowed with milk and honey." He desired *the Lord Himself* to be in their midst. Therefore, instead of being excited about "the blessings" ahead, he began to mourn. He took the tabernacle and set it up outside the camp. Then he prayed,

> *"Show me now Your way, that I may know You, and that I may find grace in Your sight. And consider that this nation is Your people."* Exodus 33:13b NKJV

The Lord responded and said,

> *"My Presence will go with you, and I will give you rest."* Exodus 33:14 NKJV

Then Moses replied,

> *"If Your Presence does not go with us, do not bring us up from here."* Exodus 33:15 NKJV

In other words, Moses said, "I do not want just the *blessings*; I desire Your *presence* in our midst, in the very center of what we are doing."

> *"For how then will it be known that Your people and I have found grace in Your sight, except You go with us? So shall we be separate, Your people and I, from all the people who are upon the face of the earth."* Exodus 33:16 NKJV

The Lord responded to Moses' desire for His presence and said to him,

> *"I will also do this thing that you have spoken: for you have found grace in My*

sight, and I know you by name." Exodus 33:17
NKJV

Moses could have been satisfied with just the promised blessings of God. But he interceded for the presence of the Lord, that God Himself would be in their midst. The Lord saw that He was valued, and wanted, and He remained.

We see this same principle of the Lord being constrained in Luke 24:15-32. Following His resurrection, Jesus was walking with His disciples but they did not realize who He was yet. Jesus shared from the scriptures concerning Himself, then He started to go. But they constrained Him, saying, "abide with us." So, rather than leaving, He tarried with them. Later their eyes "opened" and they knew it was Jesus.

Our God is a seeking God. Yet He comes in only where He is wanted, then further makes Himself known. He is seeking those today who would hear His knock and desire His presence.

> *"Behold, I stand at the door, and knock: if any man hear my voice, and open the door, I will*

come in to him, and will sup with him, and he with me." Revelation 3:18

May we be as Moses, who interceded for the presence of the Lord in an intense desire that the Lord come and remain. May we never become satisfied with just the things of God, but always value His presence, loving Him above all else.

"Parousia" is a New Testament Greek word that relates to the Second Coming of Christ; this word also relates to the *"Presencing"* of the Lord, in which He is beginning to reveal Himself in a greater and more personal way to those who have come apart to seek Him.

Today, we can believe for His "presencing" in greater ways. May we live our lives in inner communion with Him. May the beauty of a life deeply embedded with worship mark our lives also. There is a relationship that is available, a growing love relationship with the Lord.

My prayer is simply this, teach us Lord, the ways of Your presence...

Our Need for a Present Word

"We know not what we should pray."
Romans 8:26

Recently, as I was in prayer for a need that had been shared with me, I thought I knew how to pray: I was familiar with all the scriptures relating to that need, so I would just begin to pray them!

Much to my surprise, as I began to get quiet before the Lord, He led me in a whole new direction. Scripture after scripture came before me, as my prayer time turned into a prayerful little Bible study.

As I thought on the significance of the words that the Holy Spirit was quickening, I began to realize how essential it is that we have a "present word" from the Lord. Whether praying or speaking, we need to hear from the Lord, in order to speak forth His word, quickened and anointed, that His Spirit and life might flow through us.

Had I not heard from the Lord, I might have done a lot of praying, but I would have missed what was necessary to unlock the door for living faith to enter. How easy it is to miss! We can spend a lot of time that may not be fruitful time, even in our religious endeavors. How dependent we are on the Holy Spirit for accomplishing anything of Kingdom value!

How do we come up into a *higher level of spiritually hearing* from the Lord?

The enlargement of our spiritual capacity begins and continues to grow through *spiritual hunger*, as I simply become *awakened* to the love song of the Lord and begin to respond.

> *"The song of songs, which is Solomon's."*
> Song of Solomon 1:1

As I come to experience His love, I realize it is more than anything this world can offer, and I begin to desire it above all else. From that initial hunger, something in me starts to cry out for more of Him, as I make a commitment to follow after Him.

"Draw me, we will run after thee: the king hath brought me into his chambers: we will be glad and rejoice in thee, we will remember thy love more than wine: the upright love thee." Song of Solomon 1:4

As I continue to seek after the Lord, instead of becoming simply "satisfied," a "dissatisfied satisfaction" starts to grow inside me.

I begin to realize that I have found the one pearl of great price, and I become willing to "sell all" to obtain it (Matthew 13:46). I realize it is a treasure hid in a field, and I must buy the whole field to obtain it (Matthew 13:44). This is not a Sunday morning thing; it involves every aspect of my life!

Yet, as I become willing and yielded to the Lord, a transformation is set in motion inside me, where now it is no longer my life, but His life in me that is beginning to govern my choices and the things I say or do (Galatians 2:20).

As I experience His life inside me, a further hunger is released; something within me begins to stretch as I cry out for more and more of Him.

> *"Tell me, O thou whom my soul loveth, where thou feedest, where thou makest thy flock to rest at noon: for why should I be as one that turneth aside by the flocks of thy companions?"* Song of Solomon 1:7

As I continue to steadfastly seek after the Lord, not out of mere religious requirement, but out of a love relationship, something within me *awakens to His voice*, as I learn to commune and fellowship with Him.

The apostle John speaks of this fellowship which he enjoyed and wished we would have too, a *fellowship* that is *"with the Father, and with His Son Jesus Christ"* (1 John 1:3).

> *"The voice of my beloved! behold, he cometh leaping upon the mountains, skipping upon the hills ... My beloved spake, and said unto me, Rise up, my love, my fair one, and come*

away … Arise, my love, my fair one, and come away." Song of Solomon 2:8,10,13

As the Lord brings me into that place of *hearing His heart*, notice that the call to "come away" is repeated twice in the above passage, to come apart for quality fellowship with Him.

Jesus echoed the same desire when He ordained twelve "that they should be with Him" so that *He* might send them forth (Mark 3:13-15). In today's methodology, how easy it is to miss this most important key to the fulfillment of the high call of God resting on our lives.

As I come into that place of being with Him in quality times alone, while also maintaining continued fellowship with Him as I am doing my duties, I come into a poise of spirit where the Lord is able to share His heart with me, including His heart for others.

From that place of simply *learning to know His heart*, will come a higher level of spiritual hearing: the right word, at the right time, in the right situation, for the right person.

"We have a little sister ... what shall we do for our sister in the day when she shall be spoken for? If she be a wall, we will build upon her a palace of silver: and if she be a door, we will inclose her with boards of cedar." Song of Solomon 8:8-9

"A man hath joy by the answer of his mouth: and a word spoken in due season, how good is it!" Proverbs 15:23

In Isaiah 50:4, Isaiah speaks of the Lord *awakening our ear* "morning by morning." There is no one-time experience of the Lord that will bring me into this or carry me through the days ahead. Day by day, as I come into His presence, He "opens" my ear.

Psalm 40:6 speaks of this "opening" of the ear. The King James says, *"Mine ears hast thou opened."* My margin translates the word "opened" as "digged." Mine ears hast thou digged!

I love how the Amplified Bible paraphrases this same verse. *"You have given me the capacity to hear and obey."* The Lord has given all of us this capacity. As we are willing to allow Him to "dig out" all that would hinder and release within us all that He is, He will impart into our spirit all we need, day by day.

> *"Now we have received ... the spirit which is of God; that we might know the things that are freely given to us of God."* 1 Corinthians 2:12

John the Baptist, a prophetic voice in a transitional time, was the "voice of one" crying out in the wilderness of that day. What he was declaring went beyond the existing religious expectation; his voice prepared a way not only for the Lord to come, but for a people to recognize His coming and enter into the new day at hand.

We are living in a very critical time, again, a transitional time. How important it is that we come into a place of direct communion with the Lord and learn to be led by His Holy Spirit.

How the Lord longs to release Himself within us, that we might become the very embodiment of who He is, enabling others to see and know Him not just through our words, but through our lives.

> *"Herein is our love made perfect, that we may have boldness in the day of judgment: because as he is, so are we in this world."* 1 John 4:17

There is an end-time witness, a people who are carriers of His presence, who the Lord is raising up. This requires a purity of life, that we might become as a "sea of glass," transparent, with nothing to hide. A tiny bit of mixture taints the whole glass. A sail set just a little to the left or right can change the whole course of a ship.

The dealings of God are intense within those who are sold out and determined to go all the way with the Lord. He is preparing them not only to be a voice, but to be a manifestation of His presence and glory beyond what has yet been seen through the church age.

"For whom the Lord loveth he chasteneth, and scourgeth every son whom he receiveth." Hebrews 12:6

In that manifestation of His glory and presence will come a releasing of authority through lives that have been broken: broken of all self-will; broken of all strong opinionatedness; broken of reactions; not moved by acceptance or rejection; broken, that Christ might be heard and seen as He shines forth from within. These are those who are coming up from the wilderness "leaning" on their beloved (Song of Solomon 8:5).

"To whom God would make known what is the riches of the glory of this mystery among the Gentiles; which is Christ in you, the hope of glory." Colossians 1:27

We are living in a transitional time. Those who are prepared, the Lord is about to bring beyond the gifting of the church age and into the governmental rule of His reign. He is coming to be seen and admired in His saints, those who believe, and to be glorified in all those who have appropriated His grace that they might walk worthy of this calling (2 Thessalonians 1:10-12).

We recently received encouragement that a new day was dawning, and the Spirit of the Lord would cause His people to gather together and seek Him as never before; that a separation would come of the lukewarm from the hot, and there would come a difference in the church, bringing many souls into the Kingdom.

Jesus said that His house would be called a "house of prayer" (Matthew 21:13). Yet, what percentage of time in the total program of today's average church is spent in prayer? The building of that house of prayer is about to move forward as many churches are drawn into increased times of prayer.

But it will not be just man's thoughts being prayed. It will be the prophetic releasing of God's word into circumstances and lives, bringing an alignment with God's plans and purposes, releasing revival, and opening the door for the incoming harvest.

So many see just what the world is doing. We must see what God is doing and make ourselves available to become a part. The greatest days are yet ahead for the church, as the Lord begins to release His glory.

As the Habitation of God is being established amongst His people, it is not a *visitation* we are moving toward, but a *transition* into a greater manifestation of His abiding presence.

In this presencing of the Lord, there will come the releasing of miracles we have cried out for, but have been unable to obtain through faith alone, for it has required this greater manifestation of the Lord's presence in our midst.

The Lord is "brooding" over those who are willing to "watch and wait" at the posts of His door; those who are willing to take the time "morning by morning" to be with Him, that He might lift them up into a higher spiritual realm, that they might be prepared and ready to enter in, in the coming day of His power.

> *"Blessed is the man that heareth me, watching daily at my gates, waiting at the*

posts of my doors. For whoso findeth me findeth life, and shall obtain favour of the LORD." Proverbs 8:34-35

For Kingdom fruitfulness to come forth, it is essential that we come into that place of having a "present word" from the Lord. Whether praying or speaking, we first need the guidance of the Holy Spirit.

May our hearts be open and our spirits yielded to Christ who lives within us, as we believe for the Lord to lift us up into His higher purposes, preparing us, that we might fully enter into that which He is doing in our day.

May our ears be open, to hear and understand, as we yield our lives to Him.

Times of Fellowship with the Lord

"And he that searcheth the hearts knoweth what is the mind of the Spirit, because he maketh intercession for the saints according to the will of God." Romans 8:27

The Lord blessed David and me with forty years of marriage before the Lord took him home. It was in the middle of our years of marriage that David was in Mozambique on a short-term mission trip. I was happy for him to be there, as I knew it was his heart's desire.

I was busy as the pastor of a church where I knew God had called us, and in my times of fellowship with the Lord as I spent time waiting in His presence, I was caught up in prayer, God's Word, and the things I was doing.

One particular day, however, such intercession came on me for David that I could hardly bear it. I remember telling our church of the intensity of it as we met that Sunday and prayed together. That intercession lasted for a couple of days, then it lifted. I remember wondering what it had been all about, as I continued on where God had me.

It was a few days later that I received a phone call. David told me he had been riding in a truck when a gunman came up the road. Standing about five feet away, the gunman aimed an AK47 at the center of his chest, then shot. The blast threw him back, so the gunman thought he hit him, and left. However, the bullet missed!

As I spoke to David on the phone, he was still in shock. I remember saying over and over to him, "But intercession came, and we were praying for you. The bullet missed!" I was overwhelmed as I remembered the intercession that had come. The faithfulness of God!

The Lord is calling us into a place of fellowship with Him. From that place of fellowship, He will give us the right prayer at the right time, the right declaration, the right word, whatever it is He has need of, as we make ourselves available for His higher purposes.

In Genesis 18, Abraham was simply sitting in the door of his tent, when the Lord came. Abraham's immediate response was to minister to the Lord.

From that place of fellowship, the Lord said, *"Should I not share with my friend Abraham that which I am about to do?"* Abraham was brought into a place of intercession for the righteous to be saved and brought out of Sodom and Gomorrah before judgment fell.

As Christians, we are in covenant relationship with the Lord Jesus Christ. Covenant is a very powerful thing. In scripture, David, when faced by enemies, prayed on the basis of covenant. An understanding of covenant brings tremendous peace and reassurance that we have a God who loves us and who will move on our behalf when we cry out to Him, be it for our own lives, or the life of another.

In more recent times, one day when I was walking in the Prayer Chapel, praying, intercession came and I cried out, "Oh Lord, the blood of your people. Lord, the blood of your people." In that moment, my cry went beyond my own immediate concerns or loved ones, to an expression of the very heart of God and the fellowship of His sufferings (Philippians 3:10).

As I prayed, this scripture came to mind:

> *"The LORD said, "What have you done? Listen! Your brother's blood cries out to me from the ground." Genesis 4:10 NIV*

I came to understand that there are those who have suffered and who have even died because of their faith. But their blood still speaks, and God hears those cries. For just a moment, He allowed me to share with Him in the fellowship of His sufferings.

> *"By faith Abel offered God a better sacrifice than Cain did. By faith he was commended as a righteous man, when God spoke well of his offerings. And by faith he still speaks, even though he is dead." Hebrews 11:4 NIV*

We are to practice the presence of the Lord, every moment of every day. But as we also set apart time to fellowship with the Lord, He will share His heart with us and cause us to be a part of that which He is doing today, just as He did with Abraham in his day.

Isaiah 60 speaks of gross darkness on the face of the earth. We are seeing that! Yet we are also told that His glory will arise and be seen in the midst of this darkness.

> *"For, behold, the darkness shall cover the earth, and gross darkness the people: but the LORD shall arise upon thee, and his glory shall be seen upon thee."* Isaiah 60:2

Can our prayers make a difference? Yes! We can enter into fellowship with the Lord and allow His heart to find expression through us. There is a "presencing" of the Lord that we can contend for. There is also a "word with consequences" that God is releasing, that can and will have an impact.

I remember another experience I had years ago. I was watching one of God's chosen saints suffer at the mouth of another. As I watched and listened, I went into a dialogue with the Lord. As I did, I remembered another man of God who also suffered greatly. Within myself I said to the Lord, "You don't treat those who love You very well."

As I did, suddenly, so fierce it startled me, I heard come through my mouth, "That's enough!" Instantly, the verbal beating this precious man of God was taking, stopped.

Through that experience, I came into a new realization of the power and authority of a quickened word that comes from God, as well as His fierce love over them that love Him.

The word of God is powerful! It is at His word the world was formed. Let's believe for the Lord to draw us, as never before, into times of fellowship with Him, that we might come to know His heart and speak His quickened word, as His Spirit within us moves and finds expression through our very lives.

The need is urgent. The Lord is looking today for those who would make themselves available to fellowship with Him. Will we respond by saying, "Lord, I am available," and then make the necessary choices to set aside time to be with Him?

We all have responsibilities we must fulfill, in a right way that gives glory to God. But there is other time available in our days that we can redeem, that we can spend in prayer, worship, waiting on the Lord, meditating on His Word ... watching, waiting, and listening for His guidance, that we might be available for His higher purposes.

As we set our gaze on the Lord and in yieldedness spend time with Him, we can become more sensitive and responsive to His Spirit, becoming channels through whom God can move today.

Derek Prince wrote a book, *Shaping History through Prayer and Fasting*. Just the title says a lot! Another book, *Rees Howells, Intercessor*, gives us the testimony of the impact made by Rees Howells and other intercessors who prayed during World War II.

There are many other powerful testimonies of people who lived in various places, at various times, who made an impact through prayer. As we make ourselves available to the Lord today, we too, can make a difference.

Receiving Healing

"Beloved, I wish above all things that thou mayest prosper and be in health, even as thy soul prospereth." 3 John 1:2

It seems so many are struggling with physical challenges today. How we need the healing touch of God, whether believing for ourselves or for others.

How comforting to understand that the Lord God Almighty is touched with the feelings of our infirmities, and He cares. There are many scriptures that speak of the compassion of Christ and of His heart being moved toward the needs of others.

Compassion alludes to kindness and sympathy. To feel compassion is to feel concern or sorrow for the sufferings or trouble of another, accompanied by an urge to help. Some synonyms for compassion are kindness, empathy, sympathy, benevolence, and care; all characteristic of a compassionate heart.

One scripture (There are many!) which speaks of the

compassion of Christ is Matthew 14:14, *"And Jesus went forth, and saw a great multitude, and was moved with compassion toward them, and he healed their sick."*

A familiar verse, with profound truth: *"Jesus Christ the same, yesterday, and to day, and for ever"* (Hebrews 13:8). As seen in times past in scripture, so today, the heart of God is moved as we cry out to Him in our need.

The Apostle Peter encourages us: *"Finally, all of you, be like-minded, be sympathetic, love one another, be compassionate and humble"* (1 Peter 3:8 NIV).

Even as Christ's heart is touched by the needs of others, so are we to have compassionate hearts and learn to share in His love, intercession, and care for others. A compassionate heart is something we can pray and believe for!

As friends have needs or prayer requests come, or we may just be walking down the street and see the need of another, how often I find myself praying for healing, intervention, God's touch.

Scripture tells us God is touched with the feelings of our infirmities:

> *"For we have not an high priest which cannot be touched with the feeling of our infirmities."* Hebrews 4:15

Yet not only does God have compassion, *He is able* to help!

> *"Wherefore he is able also to save them to the uttermost that come unto God by him, seeing he ever liveth to make intercession for them."* Hebrews 7:25

> *"He is able (immediately) to run to the cry of (assist, relieve) those who are being tempted and tested and tried (and who therefore are being exposed to suffering)."* Hebrews 2:18b AMPC

We are encouraged, *"Let us therefore come boldly unto the throne of grace, that we may obtain mercy, and find grace to help in time of need"* (Hebrews 4:16 KJV).

God's love is immeasurable (Ephesians 3:19; Romans 8:39). With confidence, we can come before His throne, whether for fellowship or with a need, believing into His power, His finished work on Calvary, His compassion, and His love.

When we pray for healing, whether for ourselves or for another, it is good to remember that God created our bodies to heal. There are many ways God works in healing. Obviously, it is important!

I am thankful for the medical profession, that our bodies can be studied and we can cooperate with healing. I am thankful for the natural things we can do through diet and exercise, to strengthen our bodies. I am thankful for times when the power of God touches us, bringing healing beyond what good care or time alone would bring.

When I have a need, I like to spend time with the Healer, the Lord Jesus Christ. I will lift my need before Him, then leave it there, at His feet, as I go on to worship and fellowship with Him.

"The power of the Lord was present to heal them." Luke 5:17b

I also love to spend time "soaking" in scriptures. As I listen to healing scriptures, I rest in His presence, allowing the Word of God to penetrate my heart.

"So then faith cometh by hearing, and hearing by the word of God." Romans 10:17

As we listen to scripture, read, or simply think about scriptures we are familiar with, the Word of God fills our hearts with faith.

Years ago, I strained my knees trying to carry a piece of heavy furniture down a narrow staircase. I got stuck halfway down, unable to move back up or continue down! Through a lot of straining, I eventually got the furniture down the stairs, but not without hurting my knees.

One knee hurt worse than the other. I would put my hand on the knee that hurt most, pray, then spend time worshipping the Lord, becoming like a sponge, as I soaked in His presence and healing power.

One day I noticed that knee, the one that was hurt worse, was healed. And the other knee still hurt! The Lord showed me that was not a coincidence, and I began to pray for the other knee as well. Both are healed today!

More recently, I had a need I was trusting the Lord to meet. Some friends were also standing with me in prayer. One day, after a time of prayer, I felt "life" touch me. It's hard to explain, but it was a powerful experience. When "life" touched me, a turning came. Through that touch of life, I received healing and regained strength.

However the Lord heals you – through the process of time, instantly, through medical care, through time in His presence – the important thing is that you are healed.

I don't know why sometimes healing comes and other times we don't see it manifest as quickly as we would like. But one thing I do know is, more healing is experienced when we pray and believe, than when we don't! I believe we are going to see even greater authority and victory in the area of healing in the days ahead!

Today, may you be blessed with quality times to be in the Lord's presence. May the Word of God become rooted in your heart! May you receive life! May healing increase in your body, in every area of need. May faith fill your heart even as you read this; may the Lord touch and bless you even now.

A few scriptures I'd like to leave with you:

"So then faith cometh by hearing, and hearing by the word of God." Romans 10:17

"He sent his word, and healed them, and delivered them from their destructions." Psalm 107:20

"Bless the LORD, O my soul, and forget not all his benefits:

Who forgiveth all thine iniquities; who healeth all thy diseases;

Who redeemeth thy life from destruction;

who crowneth thee with lovingkindness and tender mercies;

Who satisfieth thy mouth with good things; so that thy youth is renewed like the eagle's."
Psalm 103:2–5

As we believe into the power and compassion of Christ, whatever the need, may we also position ourselves in the *faithfulness* of God.

"This I recall to my mind, therefore have I hope.

It is of the LORD's mercies that we are not consumed, because his compassions fail not.

They are new every morning: great is thy faithfulness.

The LORD is my portion, saith my soul; therefore will I hope in him.

The LORD is good unto them that wait for him, to the soul that seeketh him.

It is good that a man should both hope and

quietly wait for the salvation of the LORD"
Lamentations 3:21–26.

As we linger in an attitude of worship, quietly spending time in the Lord's presence, may we become receptive, like a sponge, as we open our hearts to receive healing from the Lord.

As I pray for each one who reads this book, it is my earnest, heartfelt prayer that whatever the need, the Lord will touch each one.

As you continue to spend time with Christ, the Healer, the one who loves you and gave His life for you, may He bless you in a very personal way.

Section 7
Prayer

Lord, Help Us to Pray

"Out of the same mouth proceedeth blessing and cursing. My brethren, these things ought not so to be. Doth a fountain send forth at the same place sweet water and bitter? ... so can no fountain both yield salt water and fresh."
James 3:10-12

Attitudes can hinder prayer from being effective. One example is prayer for our government. In our country we have opportunity to vote every four years. It's a time where differences flare up and conversations can become heated. Once a candidate takes office, how are we to position ourselves as Christians?

Foundational, God is sovereign. Ultimately, it is God who allows those in authority to rule.

> *"God hath spoken once; twice have I heard this; that power belongeth unto God."* Psalm 62:11

> *"By me kings reign, and princes decree justice. By me princes rule, and nobles, even all the judges of the earth."* Proverbs 8:15-16

Scripture also makes it clear we are to respect and pray for those in authority:

Peter wrote, *"Respect everyone, and love the family of believers. Fear God, and respect the king"* (1 Peter 2:17 NLT). This is pretty amazing when you remember Peter was under a rule which persecuted Christians.

Paul, also under a government that would have been easy to criticize, said, *"Everybody must obey the civil authorities that are over him, for no authority exists except by God's permission; the existing authorities have been established by Him"* (Romans 13:1 Williams Translation).

Timothy, under the same rule said,

> *"I exhort therefore, that, first of all, supplications, prayers, intercessions, and giving of thanks, be made for all men; For kings, and for all that are in authority; that we may lead a quiet and peaceable life in all godliness and honesty.*
>
> *For this is good and acceptable in the sight of God our Saviour; Who will have all men to be saved, and to come unto the knowledge of the truth."* 1 Timothy 2:1-4

Times and seasons change. In our country we have the opportunity to vote every four years. But today, I am to respect and pray for the leaders *God* has allowed, as I trust the Lord for tomorrow.

Daniel said *"And he changeth the times and the seasons: he removeth kings, and setteth up kings: he giveth wisdom unto the wise, and knowledge to them that know understanding"* (Daniel 2:21).

As I place my trust in God, my desire is to be effective in prayer. This means I have to guard my thoughts and attitudes from anything that might hinder the quality of my spiritual life and times of prayer.

On the cross, Jesus did not pray only for Himself and His friends. While He was committing His own spirit to His heavenly Father, He also prayed for those who were crucifying Him.

This is the perfect victory of the cross. Vertically, I commit myself to God. Horizontally, I pray for others.

If we want God to use us in prayer, we must be willing for God to so work in our hearts that we can pray for all of mankind, including our elected officials. We can't pray effectively and curse with the same mouth. It is easy to criticize. But am I willing to stand in the gap and pray?

In society, all the structures and roles we see are temporary. In eternity, we will be what we have become through the choices we've made as we yield to the Lord in the society we live in today. Until then, we have this pocket of time wherein we can walk uprightly before God as a testimony to others and as a witness unto Him.

May we make right choices, that we might mature and grow, that the nature of Christ might be fully formed in us. May we pray for the salvation of others. May we pray for those who are already saved, that God's purposes might be fulfilled in each life.

Sweet and bitter water cannot come from the same fountain. 1 Peter 3:7 speaks of prayer being hindered through wrong attitudes. Acts 10:31, of prayer being heard because of living righteously before God. James 5:16 tells us the prayer of a righteous man avails much!

When the disciples asked Jesus to teach them to pray, notice the teaching that follows in Matthew 6:9-13. This is also found in Luke 11:2-4.

"After this manner therefore pray ye:

Our Father which art in heaven, Hallowed be thy name.

Thy kingdom come. Thy will be done in earth, as it is in heaven.

Give us this day our daily bread.

And forgive us our debts, as we forgive our debtors.

And lead us not into temptation, but deliver us from evil:

For thine is the kingdom, and the power, and the glory, for ever. Amen."

How important we keep our spirits clear, that the Lord might use us now and, in the days ahead! As we submit ourselves to God, He is able to keep us from stumbling!

"Now unto him that is able to keep you from falling, and to present you faultless before the presence of his glory with exceeding joy,

To the only wise God our Saviour, be glory and majesty, dominion and power, both now and ever. Amen." Jude 1:24-25

Whether it be political affairs, or other matters, may we truly represent Christ and be vessels He can use, living honorable lives for His name's sake. As we maintain right attitudes may we be effective as witnesses and in our prayer closets.

Intercession

"Teach us to pray." Luke 11:1

There is an increasing travail today for the true life and ministry of Christ to be made manifest in and through lives submitted to the Lord Jesus Christ. This travail is being imparted by the Holy Spirit, to bring forth a people who will live and walk in the Spirit. These are being enabled to live overcoming lives, and to become joined with the Lord in a cooperative relationship in all that He is doing today.

John the Baptist was a singular prophetic voice in a transitional time. It is again a transitional time, but today it is a corporate prophetic voice that the Lord is bringing forth.

There is an overcoming people whom the Lord is enabling by His Holy Spirit; those who are walking in an intimate relationship with the Lord, who are coming to know the Lord and His voice and follow the leading of the Holy Spirit.

From this place of individual personal relationship with the Lord, there is coming a corporate prophetic sound. The very heart of God is finding expression in a voice who is becoming *"the voice of one"* in today's transition.

> *"And I heard as it were the voice of a great multitude, and as the voice of many waters, and as the voice of mighty thunderings, saying, Alleluia: for the Lord God omnipotent reigneth."* Revelation 19:6

There is a singular, yet corporate sound of intercession; the groanings are getting stronger and closer together, because the time of birthing is near.

There is also a singular, yet corporate sound of worship; the sound of worship which is around the throne, is starting to be heard in the earth again.

A people are being brought into the place of the throne, into governmental authority, through the submission of their lives to the Lord Jesus Christ. From that place of submission, as His throne is being established, the sounds of intercession and worship intertwine in bringing forth the new.

Worship and intercession are key to the intervention of the Lord being released into lives and circumstances. Webster defines the word "intervene" as meaning "any interference in the affairs of another." This is the Lord's desire, to "interfere" with man's plans that He might bring forth His plans.

"To intervene" also means "to come" or "lie between." The Lord is standing in between the place where we presently are and the place He is calling us to be, and He is knocking to attract our attention.

> "Behold, I stand at the door, and knock: if any man hear my voice, and open the door, I will come in to him, and will sup with him, and he with me." Revelation 3:20

Our part is to respond and open the door so the Lord can "interfere" in our lives, to bring forth His new. As I respond to the Lord, it releases His intervention into my life.

Spiritual desire opens the door and paves the way for the Lord to come intervene in our lives, churches, ministries, and circumstances, that He might be who He wants to be and do what He wants to do, in and through our lives.

We are living in a transitional time as we near the end of the dispensation of grace and approach the kingdom age. Worship and intercession are at the heart of the end-time intervention of our Lord. They are the enabling that will release and make a way for the Lord to "interfere" in our lives. We need the intervention of the Lord today in every dimension of our lives.

The Lord is calling us up into an intimacy of knowing Him, that His heart might find expression. Worship and intercession simply open the door, paving the way for His coming, that He might come in intervention, bringing forth His new.

Concerning prayer, there is much today that would try to rob us of our inner communion with the Lord. Television, music, busyness – all these challenge the devotional aspect of our lives. It is so important that we learn to govern our time wisely and also learn to maintain our inner communion with the Lord.

Scripture tells us we are to *"pray without ceasing."* I can pray when I am driving my car, cutting the grass, or shoveling snow. But I cannot pray when I am worrying, holding resentment, or preoccupied with thoughts not from God. The same part of me that prays can become busy with these other things, interfering with the fellowship I am being called to continually maintain.

There is a clearing of our lives, a faith, forgiveness, and poise of spirit toward the Lord, that He is calling us up into, that we might *"pray without ceasing."* The heavens will then open and the Lord will begin to move in the dimension He desires, and which we desperately need.

To spend quality time in prayer is my choice. When I set apart time for prayer, the Holy Spirit will bring forth the intercession of Christ in true Holy Spirit workings and movings, to bring forth His life through those who are receptive and willing.

Are we willing to clear our lives from those things that hinder? Are we willing to learn to govern our time that we might be available for His purpose?

The Lord is calling us to be a part of this corporate, prophetic, end-time sound that is coming from the throne, to be a part of bringing forth His new.

****

Lord, please help us to understand and walk worthy of Your calling.

A Day of Transition

"O taste and see that the LORD is good."
Psalm 34:8

We are approaching the birthing of a new day in the Lord. The beginnings of this transitional period are being felt as we move from the present day of grace into the new day of His Kingdom.

Regardless of where we are in the Lord's economy of time, today is the appointed time in which we can meet the Lord. As we hear and respond to the upward call of God, the Lord works within our lives according to the level of our commitment to Him.

This visitation of the Lord is not openly visible. But from within the church, the Lord is calling a people unto Himself. As we respond, there is a preparation within our lives for the critical hour in which we live, even as John the Baptist was uniquely prepared for his hour.

In Jesus' time, a transition was made from law to grace. In our day of transition, we are moving from grace into the day of His Kingdom, or the Third Day. We, as a Bride are being adorned to know Him, and then as Sons, to be made a part of His purposes both now and for all eternity.

We are not much different from His disciples who misunderstood the Lord's purposes in their day. They were so adjusted to the world system as they knew it, that they looked to the Lord for political intervention to preserve their way of life.

But Jesus had no interest in the world system of that day. His interest was in preparing a people to know Him, who would move from that economic and religious system into the new day that was before them.

To do this, as a bride, they first had to come to know Him in a deeper and more personal way. From that place of intimacy, as sons, He was then able to bring them into a functional position within His purpose.

We have changed little as we again face a time of transition. We still look to the Lord for political intervention, to preserve a present world and religious system, in which He has no interest. The Lord is yet looking for a people who would know Him, who would constrain Him to abide with them, as He leads them into the coming new day.

We are entering a season of great deception and tribulation. There is an urgent need today to personally know the Lord as never before. This level of knowing develops as we spend time with Him, not only during our daily devotional time, but throughout the day, as we learn to seek His heart in the daily circumstances of our individual lives.

Day by day, as we continue to spend quality times in the Lord's presence, then stay sensitive and responsive to His presence in our daily walk, our yearning and spiritual capacity for more of the Lord continues to grow. This spiritual hunger increasingly draws us closer to the Lord and will also carry us through the day at hand.

We can only understand what it will mean to continually abide in His presence and glory in the coming new heaven and earth, as we receive touches of being in His presence and glory today.

As His presence and His glory become a greater reality within our life experience, the desire to abide in His unveiled presence in the day before us continues to grow within our hearts. This yearning causes us to say, even as John said, *"Even so, come, Lord Jesus"* (Revelation 22:20b).

****

Come, Lord Jesus, into my life and circumstances, and carry us into this new day that is before us.

Entering Into His Rest

"Not by might, nor by power, but by my spirit..." Zechariah 4:6b

There is a present-day *intercession* for God to intervene, that His presence might be established in the midst of His people in a more *manifest* way. This intercession is being released through a people who are sold out to the Lord and desire His best at any cost.

> *"In the same way the Spirit also helps our weakness; for we do not know how to pray as we should, but the Spirit Himself intercedes for us ... He intercedes for the saints according to the will of God."* Romans 8:26-27 NASB

> *"He that loveth me shall be loved of my Father, and I will love him, and will manifest myself to him."* John 14:21b

The *intervention* of God is very real and brings *transition* when it occurs. Back in the mid-seventies, I experienced the intervention of God in my own circumstances in a very real and life-changing way. At that time, I had little understanding of intercession; I am not sure I had ever personally experienced it.

Yet, I woke in the middle of the night crying over and over, "Lord, please intervene at any cost." When it lifted, I wondered what that was all about, then went back to sleep.

What followed the next day was beyond anything I had ever experienced: I was heading south; instead, I was turned and went north. The whole course of my life was changed, and I was set on the path to where God has me today.

Any major *transition* in my life has come through the *intervention* of God or at *His initiative*. At times, there was a sense of change coming, or even a drawing to intercession.

But when transition finally occurred, it was not through my own orchestration, but God's. I simply *recognized* what God was doing and said yes, as I *yielded* to the Lord and His movements.

How we need the intervention of God today! Not just personally or in our nation, but in the church. As God's people, we have never been at a more desperate point. We need something beyond what we are presently experiencing, yet there has never been less *we* can do to make it happen!

Although I cannot cause the intervention of God to happen, I can *desire* it and *position* myself, so when it does happen, I won't miss it. This requires that I come into a sensitivity of spirit and yieldedness to the Lord.

As I yield to the Lord, I come into a place of *rest* found only in Christ Jesus. I come to know who God is and learn to trust in His sovereignty. I recognize that God has a plan and understand that He is not yet finished, but His desire will surely come forth as I wait for Him.

I recognize my helplessness, my *utter dependence* on the Lord. As I wait on Him, I am confident His plan and the unfolding of His purposes will certainly come. But I understand it will not come through human striving.

I watch and wait in an attitude of worship. Then in His perfect timing and way, His divine activity is released. A working of the Lord takes place, that which only He can do.

> "Blessed is the man that heareth me, watching daily at my gates, waiting at the posts of my doors.
>
> For whoso findeth me findeth life, and shall obtain favour of the LORD." Proverbs 8:34-35

The life-changing intervention of God that I experienced in the mid-seventies was not through any self-effort. At the time, I had no idea that I even needed a change in my circumstances. But God in His sovereignty knew.

The Lord recently brought not only that particular incident back to mind, but caused me to remember time after time, when He has *intervened* that there might come a transitioning into the new. These often were to places beyond what I even knew to hope or pray for, until the Lord revealed that next step in His plan.

Seele Kinne talks about not just an *incident*, but a *state* of intervention, a "high state of divine control," into which the Lord desires to bring those who are willing.

"...in intervention, the hand of God's power is present to carry one beyond ordinary human attainment and miraculously sets one onward into the things of God. Those whom God has led in this way into spiritual states and things, if they pay heed to His moving, He will miraculously carry into the apostolic ministry.

This is a spiritual state, in which control of the motions of being, pass out of the natural into the spiritual; this is, from the initiative of the natural man, into the initiative of the Holy Spirit — a state of being moved by the divine will. Thereby there comes a full and free entrance into the supernatural realm, or the kingdom of heaven."

The Lord is working in individual lives and establishing places today, where yielded vessels are learning to enter into this spiritual state, as they recognize and participate with the Lord in that which He is doing.

This level of relationship with the Lord is available to any who would desire to submit their lives to Him and allow

His deep inner working; making themselves available to Him for the fulfillment of His purposes today; learning to live not just in the natural realm, but in the *realm of His Spirit*; allowing the Lord to *govern* their actions and even *provide* for their needs.

"For the LORD hath chosen Zion; he hath desired it for his habitation.

This is my rest for ever: here will I dwell; for I have desired it.

I will abundantly bless her provision: I will satisfy her poor with bread. I will also clothe her priests with salvation: and her saints shall shout aloud for joy.

There will I make the horn of David to bud: I have ordained a lamp for mine anointed. His enemies will I clothe with shame: but upon himself shall his crown flourish." Psalm 132:13-18

As we transition into the day before us, surely God will move and is beginning to move in the dimension so desperately needed today.

Provision will come for all that is required to fulfill His call. That provision flows from His throne as we abide in His rest, trusting in His purposes, learning to live in union and communion with Him, following His initiative.

Because we are now in a *"fullness of time"* (see Ephesians 1:10), we in the body of Christ can expect greater times of *intervention*. This is nothing we can manipulate or orchestrate; this comes through the *initiative of God.* Our part simply is to *position* ourselves, so when it does happen, we *recognize* it and *move with it.*

How can we do this? Our times of worship, waiting on the Lord, and learning to meditate on God's Word are key to maintaining an open and sensitive spirit before the Lord.

As we *prioritize*, making quality time available to be apart, alone with the Lord, while also learning to practice His presence in our daily lives, living every moment of every day in fellowship with Him, we become more *sensitive* to the leading of the Holy Spirit, learning to *obey* His promptings. As we do, we are being brought into a greater *alignment* with the Lord and that which He is doing.

There is a *rest*, *His* rest, that the Lord would have us enter *up* into. The world is trying to plant fear and insecurity. But the Lord is saying, "*Come unto me, all ye that labour and are heavy laden, and I will give you rest*" (Matthew 11:28).

And this is My rest ... I have *chosen* Zion! I have *desired* Zion, a place of worship, for My habitation. It is here, as you abide in Me and worship Me, that you will see My provision, for it is here that My throne is established; this is where I am. It is here that you will find Me and all that you need.

As I come into this place of His rest, the *mark of His presence* will surely be on my life.

> "*I in them, and thou in me, that they may be made perfect in one; and that the world may*

know that thou hast sent me, and hast loved them, as thou hast loved me." John 17:23

From this *poise of spirit,* we can expect a noticeable increase of the *Lord's intervention* in lives and circumstances. Individual lives, as well as corporate gatherings seeking this, will be marked by prayer, worship, and the Lord's presence like never before.

In this increase of the Lord's presence will be the releasing of healing, deliverance, miracles — beyond what was available in the church age through gifts and ministries alone.

We are living in a *transitional time,* between the church age and the day of His Kingdom. There is coming a *corporate function* of the body of Christ, a releasing of anointing, as a people who are waiting, worshipping, and praying together also learn to move together in the Spirit.

Spirit-given relationships have never been more important. This becoming joined together in spirit is key to the coming move of God.

There also is a further releasing of provision, *supernatural provision*, coming. I am expecting our coal to last a little longer, the fuel in my car to go a little further, our food to feed a few more mouths, as our provision is lifted from this world's economy into God's economy, because in God's economy, there always is enough.

There has come a reduction in my life, where I'm coming to rest solely in the greatness of God. Some years ago, there was a song I played over and over again, "How Great Is Our God," sung by Chris Tomlin. I played it in English. I played it in Spanish. Over and over again, I played this song that now resonates deep inside me. As I worshipped along with the words, deeper and deeper sunk this truth: *How Great Is Our God!*

This is the *rest* the Lord is calling us up into — a deep, Spirit-given understanding of His greatness and a willingness to be totally dependent on Him.

My dad used to say, "The next time the Lord lets me down, it will be the first!" I can say the same thing. How *great* is our God! How *awesome* is our God! How much He loves those who have set their love on Him!

May we enter into His rest, as He transitions us into all that is yet ahead.

Hidden Ministry

"But when thou doest alms, let not thy left hand know what thy right hand doeth: That thine alms may be in secret: and thy Father which seeth in secret himself shall reward thee openly." Matthew 6:3-4

Here Jesus speaks of a principle relating to our performing good deeds — *why*, as well as the *way*, we do what we do. "Alms" speak of giving to others as an act of virtue. We are to give to be seen by God, not by man. God, who sees in secret, will reward openly.

Yet this principle relates to more than the giving of finances or goods; it extends to the giving of our lives in whatever way God would ask of us.

For many years I was in ministry that was visible and easy to see. Whether in the pulpit or in the classroom, there was a title and role that defined me. On the mission field, it was easy to write newsletters showing pictures and giving reports of things done.

Yet, as I write this, none of these places are the primary position God has me now. There is a quiet place apart, where the Lord seems to delight to come for times of communion and fellowship.

In that hidden place, there is a quiet visitation marked by the presence of the Lord. A fresh infilling and preparation is taking place not just in me, but in all those who would come into this "quiet place" with Him.

This quiet place is not always recognized by man, but it is seen by God. John Wright Follette said, "This is the day of exhibition, exploitation, and show. How man is struggling to be seen, heard, felt, and known!"

Yet the Holy Spirit does not speak of Himself (John 16:13). He speaks only of Christ and glorifies Him. May we too, be willing to come into that place where it is not our name, but Christ who is exalted. May that which is born of the Spirit be conceived. It may manifest itself in ways that never identify us, but it will be in ways God sees and will reward.

In a day when so many are building names and ministries, may we be willing to quietly invest ourselves in simply encouraging another in their walk with the Lord. Encouragement to spend time in the Word, to spend time in prayer, that they might come into their own place of spiritual hearing and understanding.

There is a corporate sound coming forth; it is the sound of many waters (Revelation 1:15; 19:6). As you hear and I hear, we begin to harmonize in the heavenlies. God is about to move on the earth as never before. The Lord is preparing us to be a part of this great outpouring.

May we find our place in Christ and there abide. May that which is born of the Spirit find expression through us, as we each are faithful in the place God has called us to be.

Wherever God has called you, I encourage you to find time to spend in the secret place with Him. Spend time in His Word. Be faithful! The Lord will reward and bless you. "Little is much if God is in it." The reward is for faithfulness! May our desire be to hear "well done" at the end of this life (Matthew 25:21-23).

If it were a mere formula, I could tell you what to pray and when to say it. But it is a *relationship* the Lord is calling us up into, a life led by the Holy Spirit.

There will be confirming voices, pieces that fit together as we join with others also seeking after the Lord. But there is no substitute for our own time and fellowship with Him.

Through the regeneration of the Holy Spirit, we have been born again (Titus 3:5). May we come into that life we now have in Christ Jesus, living it to the fullest (Galatians 2:20).

May the One who "sees in secret" bless and strengthen you today!

Conclusion

As we conclude Book One of the *Spiritual Food for Spiritual Growth* series, we encourage you to also read Book Two, *Walking in His Ways*, which begins with Divine Guidance.

Also, we would like to speak a blessing over your life that was first spoken by my dad, Wade Taylor. We feel the Lord would have us continue to speak this blessing:

> *May you increasingly prosper, both spiritually and in your life circumstances, beyond all that you have experienced in the past, and also, may you be blessed in life, in health, and in all that is before you.*

Prayerfully yours,

Nancy Taylor Tate

Parousia Ministries
www.wadetaylor.org

Books by
Nancy Taylor Tate

That I Might Know Him

Spiritual Food for Spiritual Growth – Book One

Walking In His Ways

Spiritual Food for Spiritual Growth – Book Two

For More Deeper Life Teachings:

Please visit our ministry website, www.wadetaylor.org.

For Ministry Contact:

Please visit our ministry website, www.wadetaylor.org,
for our contact information.

Made in United States
North Haven, CT
26 December 2022

30170887R00124